W9-BMP-589

over 50
STORAGE BUILDINGS
& DECK PLANS
and do-it-yourself manual

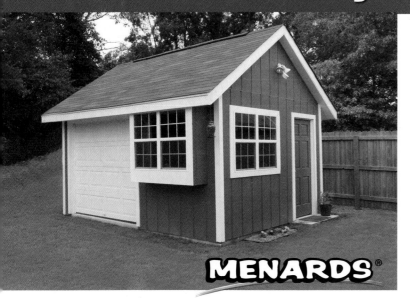

MENARDS®

Introduction

The cost of labor and materials is rising constantly. People are turning to do-it-yourself projects as a means of completing additions and renovations to their houses. If you are a homeowner, a deck or storage building can significantly increase the value of your property. You will also appreciate the additional storage space and/or living space that it provides. This book will enable you to make a new deck or storage building a reality if you follow the instructions carefully. Should you ever decide to sell your home, a carefully planned and constructed deck or storage building will add considerably to its resale value.

Over 50 Storage Buildings & Deck Plans and Do-It-Yourself Manual is a unique guide that concentrates on the process of building rather than designing. Certainly all the elements of design and proper plan detailing are considered, but this is foremost a book that graphically demonstrates the latest in construction techniques. Each step of the construction process is illustrated in detail. Several design alternatives are presented for your consideration. You will understand the construction terminology used in this book as you progress. A Glossary is provided on pages 49-51 to explain unfamiliar terms. Study the cutaway drawings and captions shown to help you envision your project. Every effort has been made at the time of publication to ensure the accuracy of the information contained herein. However, the reader should check for his or her own assurance and must be responsible for design, selection and use of suppliers, materials and actual construction.

Technical Specifications - At the time the construction drawings were prepared, every effort was made to ensure that these plans and specifications meet nationally recognized building codes (BOCA, Southern Building Code Congress and others). Because national building codes change or vary from area to area some drawing modifications and/or the assistance of a professional designer or architect may be necessary to comply with your local codes or to accommodate specific building site conditions. We advise you to consult with your local building official for information regarding codes governing your area.

ON THE COVER The storage building shown on the cover is Plan #M05-002D-4506 and is featured on page 117. Photo courtesy of HDA, Inc., St. Louis, MO.

OVER 50 STORAGE BUILDINGS & DECK PLANS AND DO-IT-YOURSELF MANUAL is published by HDA, Inc. (Home Design Alternatives), 944 Anglum Road, St. Louis, MO, 63042. All rights reserved. Reproduction in whole or in part without written permission of the publisher is prohibited. Printed in the U.S.A. © 2007.

Current Printing 5 4 3 2 1

"Thanks to MENARDS®, finding my own deck or storage building has never been easier."

Thinking about building your own deck or storage building? Perhaps you are interested in a mini-barn or garden storage? Choosing the right deck or storage building can be a daunting task.

This book has been designed to make the search simple and easy. Browse these pages and look for the style and size that best suits you and your families' needs. There are also many helpful manuals for building your own deck or storage building step-by-step. These plans have been chosen from top designers from across the country and can provide you with the perfect plan that will truly be a useful space for your whole family for years to come. You will find the expected beauty you want and the functional efficiency you need, all designed with un-matched quality.

MENARDS® state-of-the-art computerized Design-It® Center allows you to choose from a large selection of pre-priced decks or storage buildings or design your own. Easy-to-use touch screens make choosing or design-ing a deck or storage building simple. Free estimates and printouts are available within minutes.

When you have made your decision, partner with any MENARDS® friendly building material team member. They will be able to assist you in ordering the plans, choosing accessories, ordering materials, and delivering the items needed to construct your new deck or storage building.

You've found your dream storage building or deck, now what?

Follow these simple steps:

1. Review your choices below to decide what type of plan package you need.
2. To order, call or visit any MENARDS store and go to the Building Materials Desk.

To locate the MENARDS store nearest you go to **www.Menards.com**, click on Store Service then click on the Store locator.

Artist drawings and photos shown in this publication may vary slightly from the actual working drawings. Some photos are shown in mirror reverse. Please refer to the floor plan for accurate layout.

Blueprint SKU Pricing

Price Code		1-Set	Additional Sets	Reproducible Masters
P3	Menards SKU	195-9950	195-9990	195-9970
	Discount Price	$15.00	$10.00	$65.00
P4	Menards SKU	195-9951	195-9990	195-9971
	Discount Price	$20.00	$10.00	$70.00
P5	Menards SKU	195-9952	195-9990	195-9972
	Discount Price	$25.00	$10.00	$75.00
P6	Menards SKU	195-9953	195-9990	195-9973
	Discount Price	$30.00	$10.00	$80.00

Plan prices are subject to change without notice.
Please note that plans are not refundable.

Mirror Reverse	
Menards SKU	194-4327
Discount Price	$15

Express Delivery	
Menards SKU	194-4356
Discount Price	$40

Express Delivery - Most orders are processed within 24 hours of receipt. Please allow 7-10 business days for delivery. If you need to place a rush order, please call or visit any Menards store to order by 11:00 a.m. Monday-Friday CST and specify you would like express service (allow 1-2 business days).

Technical Assistance - If at any time you feel you may need assistance in the field while building, HDA offers a technical assistance line for answering building questions pertaining to your specific plan. Please call 314-770-2228 Monday-Friday between 8:00am and 5:00pm CST and our professional design staff will be happy to help.

Your Choices

The One-Set Study Package*

We offer a One-Set plan package perfect if you do not plan on modifying the original drawings. It is possible to build from a One-Set on smaller projects, but keep in mind that additional sets will be needed on larger plans for the bank, electrician, plumber or any other subcontractors you are utilizing. Also, it is a copyright violation to reproduce blueprints.

Reproducible Masters

If you wish to make some minor design changes, you'll want to order reproducible masters. These drawings contain the same information as the blueprints but are printed on reproducible paper that is easy to alter and clearly indicates your right to copy or reproduce. This will allow your builder or a local design professional to make the necessary drawing changes without the major expense of redrawing the plans. This package also allows you to print copies of the modified plans as needed. The right of building only one structure from these plans is licensed exclusively to the buyer. You may not use this design to build a second or multiple dwelling(s) without purchasing another blueprint. Each violation of the Copyright Law is punishable in a fine.

Please note: All blueprints are printed in response to your order, so we cannot honor requests for refunds. However, if for some reason you find that the plan you have purchased does not meet your requirements, you may exchange that plan for another plan in our collection within 90 days of purchase. At the time of the exchange, you will be charged a processing fee of 25% of your original plan package price, plus the difference in price between the plan packages (if applicable) and the cost to ship the new plans to you. Keep in mind, reproducible drawings can only be exchanged if the package is unopened.

TABLE OF CONTENTS

General Information

Deck Manual
Table of Contents

Storage Building Manual
Table of Contents

Build Your Own Deck? The answer is YES! By planning and doing all or part of the work yourself, you can have the deck you might not otherwise be able to afford. By supplying the labor and buying materials yourself, construction costs can be cut significantly.

Framing out a deck is not difficult. Standardized materials and construction techniques make it relatively easy if you take time to plan and work carefully. The key to a successful deck project is planning! Once you have begun construction of your deck, it is both costly and time-consuming to correct errors. So the motto of the Do-It-Yourself deck builder must be **PLAN AHEAD!** Whether you choose to draw the plans for your deck following the guidelines in this manual or you decide to purchase a pre-drawn deck plan that can be adapted to your specific requirements, you must carefully plan all elements of your deck project.

Read all the techniques and tips in this book carefully before you begin construction. It will help you determine the work you can handle alone and also where expert help might be needed. You can also learn many construction basics by studying existing decks.

Here is a checklist of design information which you must gather before you begin to design your deck:

❑ **Local Building Requirements** - Visit your local building department and determine how local building codes and zoning ordinances will influence your project. Be prepared to apply for a building permit once you have completed your design.

❑ **Deed Restrictions** - Are there conditions in your property deed that restrict the type and location of your deck? Are you planning to place your deck over property controlled by an easement for right-of-way or utility access?

❑ **Climatic Factors** - You need to determine specific climatic conditions on your property. For example, what is the maximum soil frost depth at your site? What is the prevailing wind direction during the season when your deck will receive maximum use? How much snow load will your deck have to carry during the winter months? Finally, evaluate the microclimate of your intended deck location. Microclimate includes the shading effects of deciduous or evergreen trees and shrubs, the angle of the sun in relation to nearby landscaping during different seasons, soil drainage conditions, and prevailing wind and temperature conditions.

❑ **Deck Functions** - What do you want your deck to do? Will your deck serve as an extension of a room in your home? Do you see your deck as a social gathering spot or as a place of seclusion from your neighbors? Do you want your deck to perform a special function such as containing a built-in barbecue or supporting a portable spa or hot tub?

❑ **Your Budget** - You must determine an estimated dollar amount that you plan to spend on your deck. Do you plan to construct the deck yourself or will you subcontract with a professional to build the deck after you have purchased materials? Perhaps you want a contractor to complete your deck project in its entirety. It is helpful if you can set upper and lower spending limits so that you can consider options in the materials that you plan for your deck. If you decide to finance your deck project, don't forget to include interest cost in the total cost amount.

❑ **Your Materials Source** - After you have completed your design work and have settled on a bill of materials, you should remember that Menards is an invaluable resource for the successful completion of your deck project. Consult with the Menards Building Materials Desk to check for all the materials you require. If special ordering is necessary, determine lead times for the materials. Don't underestimate the importance of a reputable resource like Menards in providing both quality materials and design knowledge.

The deck site plans on this page are included to exemplify how your deck can serve as an extension of the living space in your home. Consider first how you want to access your deck – which rooms in particular should provide entry to your deck space. Do you currently have enough door openings to handle the traffic on your deck? Perhaps you need to install additional patio doors to provide more than one access point.

If you are planning a deck that is attached to your home, you must carefully evaluate the use of door and window openings to integrate the deck with your home. Multiple access points open your deck to the interior living space of your home. For example, Figure 6A illustrates a wrap-around deck that you can access from the dining room or the sun room area.

If you are fortunate enough to be able to construct a large deck like those illustrated in Figures 6B and 6C, you will increase the total usable living area of your home significantly by careful planning and deck design. These decks add extremely useful square footage that can serve multiple functions – a simple recreation space, an outdoor dining and entertainment area, or a happy place to get away and relax.

Decks provide a sense of openness to the living space of your home. However, you can also create an enclosed, private environment with a deck that adjoins two exterior walls. In Figure 6D, observe how the modest rectangular deck links the living room and the family room while the walls of those rooms provide protection from the elements and privacy.

Figure 6B

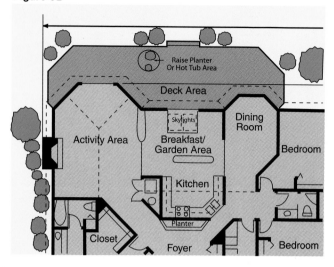

Figure 6C

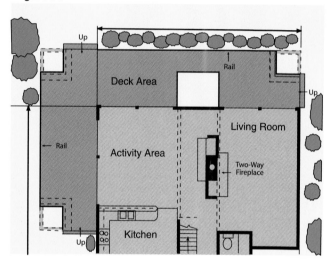

Figure 6A

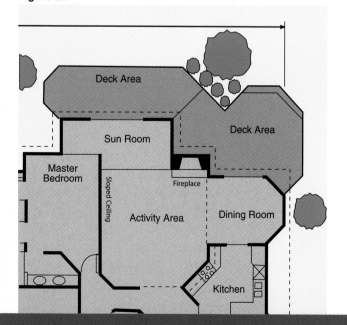

Figure 6D

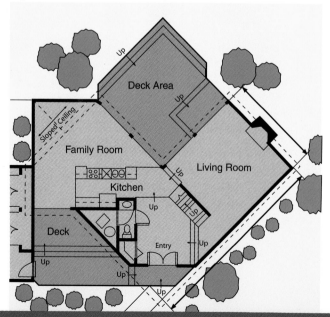

Low-Level Attached Deck
Plan #M05-107D-3002

Multi-Level Attached Deck
Plan #M05-107D-3001

Expandable Decks
Plan #M05-002D-3002

Multi-Level Detached Deck
Plan #M05-002D-3009

Free-Standing Low-Level Deck
Plan #M05-002D-3021

Multi-Level Raised Deck
Plan #M05-002D-3020

Deck With Attached Gazebo
Plan #M05-002D-3029

Low-Level Shaded Deck
Plan #M05-002D-3025

Basic Pier Block Deck

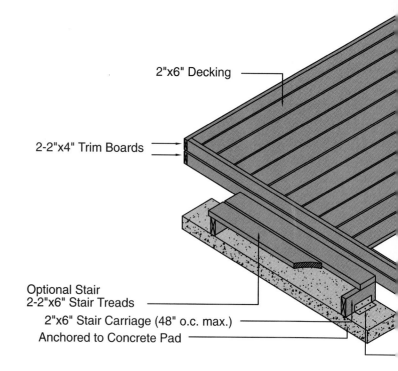

2"x6" Decking

2-2"x4" Trim Boards

Optional Stair
2-2"x6" Stair Treads
2"x6" Stair Carriage (48" o.c. max.)
Anchored to Concrete Pad

Standard Level Deck

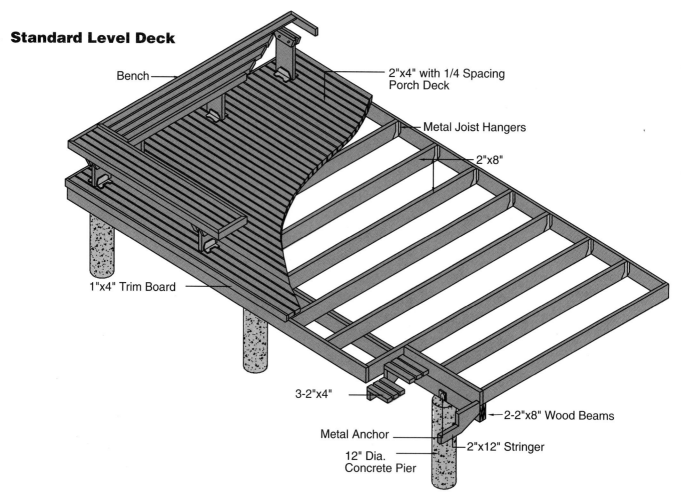

Bench

2"x4" with 1/4 Spacing
Porch Deck

Metal Joist Hangers

2"x8"

1"x4" Trim Board

3-2"x4"

2-2"x8" Wood Beams

Metal Anchor

2"x12" Stringer

12" Dia.
Concrete Pier

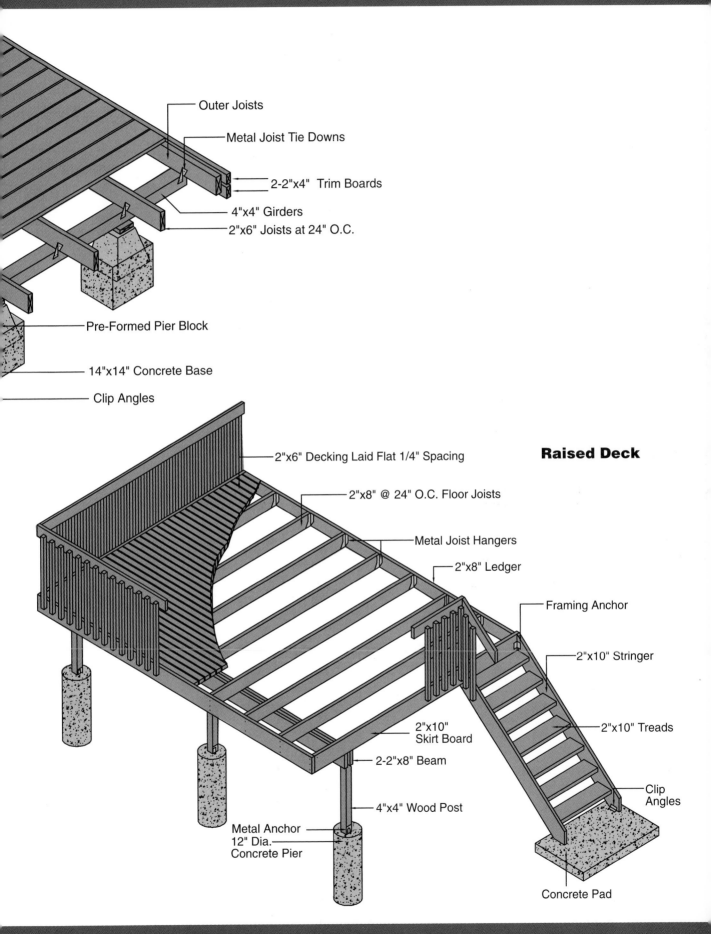

Outer Joists

Metal Joist Tie Downs

2-2"x4" Trim Boards

4"x4" Girders

2"x6" Joists at 24" O.C.

Pre-Formed Pier Block

14"x14" Concrete Base

Clip Angles

Raised Deck

2"x6" Decking Laid Flat 1/4" Spacing

2"x8" @ 24" O.C. Floor Joists

Metal Joist Hangers

2"x8" Ledger

Framing Anchor

2"x10" Stringer

2"x10" Treads

2"x10" Skirt Board

2-2"x8" Beam

4"x4" Wood Post

Clip Angles

Metal Anchor
12" Dia.
Concrete Pier

Concrete Pad

Obtain the Correct Drawing Tools

Pre-drawn deck plans are available on pages 100-115. These drawings include all the necessary information needed when building your deck. If you prefer to try your hand at designing a deck of your own, the tools you will need to draw plans for your deck are available at your local craft, art supply or variety store. You should obtain a transparent plastic ruler to help you keep your drawings to scale. Scale is a system of representation in plan drawing where small dimensions represent an equivalent large dimension. Scale is typically expressed as an equation such as 1/4"=1'-0". Better than a simple ruler is an architect's scale that calibrates dimensions directly to the scale used on your drawing. You can read 5'-0" at 1/4" scale directly on the architect's scale rather than multiplying 5 x 1-1/4" and measuring to scale with your ruler.

Also purchase two transparent right angle triangles that help to measure angles and keep your work square. You should obtain a 6"-45 degree triangle and a 6"-30/60 degree triangle. Use a medium lead pencil to draw your plans and have an eraser at hand – you will need it to correct inevitable revisions. We have provided graph paper in this manual at two different scales for your convenience. Finally, you'll need a 25-foot measuring tape to obtain outside dimensions that you will draw to scale in your deck plans.

Measuring the Site

With your 25-foot measuring tape you can begin to measure the site. Place construction stakes at the perimeter of your imaginary deck. If you are building an attached deck, use the house wall as an initial reference point. Then start to transfer measurements from your deck outline to paper. It is standard practice to orient your base plan drawing with north at the top of the plan. You should include on your base plan all surrounding elements which could influence the final design of your deck – paths or doorways which will provide access to the deck, deck views and privacy considerations, trees and their shadow patterns, other buildings, grade conditions, and any nearby underground utility services.

Finalizing the Design

Once you have transferred your site measurements into the base plan, you can begin to use the base plan to help you create the final drawings for your deck. Carefully study all the elements of the base plan and resolve any final decisions concerning deck size, height, placement, and type of pier construction.

Figure 10 - Side View of Deck Framing

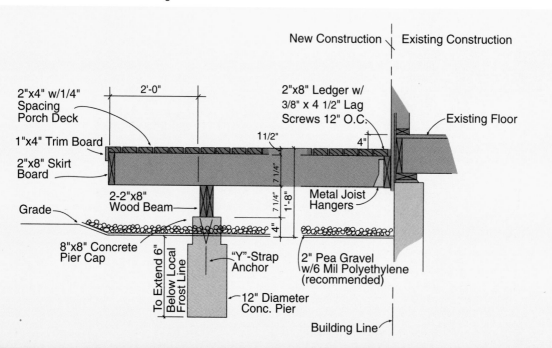

Pier Location Plan

Once you have decided on a final design, you first need to draw a pier location plan that shows the exact placement of the piers in relation to the deck outline and the existing structure if you are building an attached deck. Consult the span charts on pages 13-14 to be certain that your piers are not spaced too far apart for the joist and beam spacing that you have selected.

Deck Framing Plan

Based on the pier location plan, you will draw a deck framing plan that shows exact measurements for the joists and girders on your deck. Some designers find it easier to draw one plan for joist framing and another for girder framing. Remember to consult the table of nominal versus actual dimensions of dimensional lumber (see chart on page 19) when you calculate exact lengths of joists and girders. Again consult the span charts on pages 13-14 to ensure that you have not exceeded maximum design values for joist and girder spans.

Deck Plan

Using your deck framing plan, draw the surface of your deck as it will appear in a bird's eye view from the top. This plan will help you estimate the amount of decking (see chart on page 18), railing, and stair material required to complete your deck.

Deck Elevations

You've drawn the layers of your deck construction from the top view when you made the pier location plan, deck framing plan, and deck plan. Using those top-view plans as a guide, you then draw your deck in a sideways view – as deck elevations, which show your deck as it will appear from front, back, left, and rear sides.

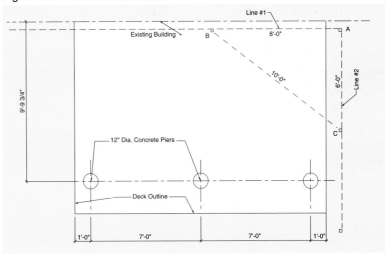

Figure 10A - Pier Location Plan

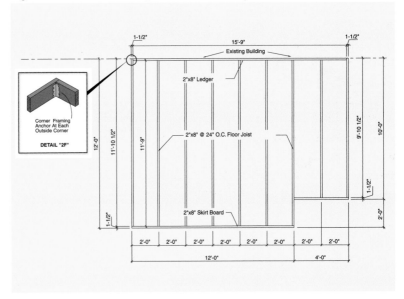

Figure 10B - Deck Framing Plan

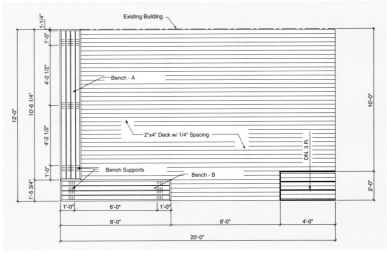

Figure 10C - Deck Plan

Once you have drawn the surface of your deck in a plan view, you must design the deck's supporting substructure. The tables on pages 13-14 will assist you in planning the critical substructure system of your deck. You should be aware that these tables reflect spans and spacings for a total load of 60 pounds per square foot, which in many localities is the current load requirement for decks mandated by the Uniform Building Code. The total load of 60 P.S.F. has two component loads – the first of 10 P.S.F. "dead" load plus a second of 50 P.S.F. "live" load. While the 60 P.S.F. total load is more than adequate for most substructure designs, special circumstances such as heavy snow loads or the weight of a hot tub will require consultation with a design professional.

Your own local building department may or may not support the 60 P.S.F. total load requirement. Again we strongly advise you to consult with your local building department to ensure that your deck substructure will meet local codes.

How to Use Deck Spans and Spacings Tables

Use the tables on pages 13-14 to plan the substructure of your deck. First determine the species group of the lumber you will use to build the substructure of your deck. If you are planning to use two different lumber species (such as Douglas fir for joists and redwood for posts, beams, and decking), don't forget to use the correct species group in each appropriate chart.

Refer to the illustrated dimensions in Figure 12 below as a graphic guide to the dimensions listed in the tables. For example, Dimension "A" refers to the maximum allowable span for decking boards listed in the Decking Span Table. Dimension "B" measures both joist span and beam spacing which are different names for an identical dimension. Dimension "C" reflects beam spans for a given beam size. Dimension "D" shows the minimum post size required to support a given load area (which you calculate by multiplying). Dimension "B" by Dimension "C"). Remember that these spans are for solid beams rather than built-up beams. A 4x6 beam (measuring 3-1/2" x 5-1/2") has greater load carrying strength than a beam built from nailing together two 2x6s (measuring 3" x 5-1/2").

Design the Substructure CAREFULLY

In planning the substructure of your deck, remember that you are working with a complex set of variables and that your final design will reflect a choice between competing alternatives. For example, if you increase the number of concrete piers you can reduce joist spans and girder size and spans. However, if your local frost line requires that piers be constructed to a depth of 3 feet, you might want to reduce the number of piers and increase joist and beam spans. Determine a solution that is cost-effective but does not compromise the strength and durability of your deck. A deck that is inadequately supported by its substructure is dangerous and will require costly repairs at a later date.

Figure 12 - Deck Substructure

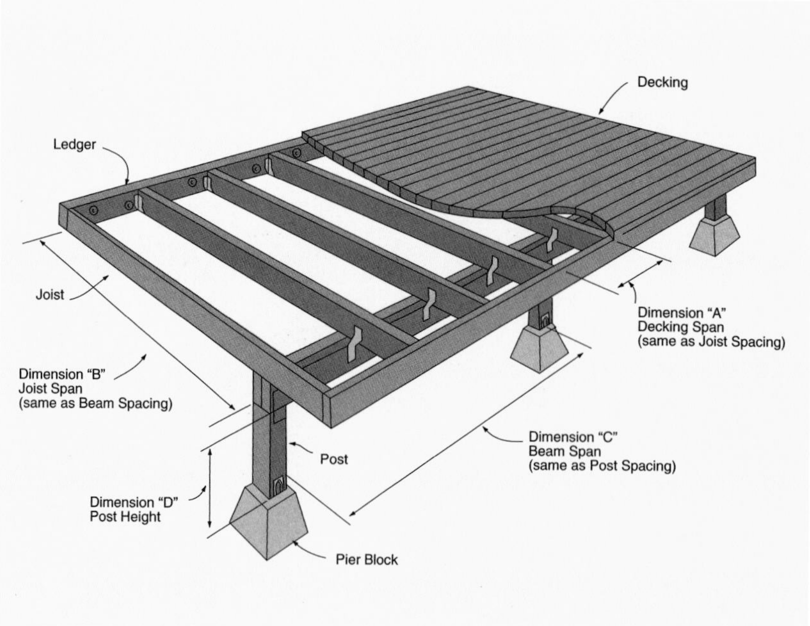

Decking

Ledger

Joist

Dimension "B"
Joist Span
(same as Beam Spacing)

Dimension "D"
Post Height

Post

Pier Block

Dimension "A"
Decking Span
(same as Joist Spacing)

Dimension "C"
Beam Span
(same as Post Spacing)

Charts are Based on a 60 P.S.F. Total Load
50 P.S.F. Live Load Plus 10 P.S.F. Dead Load

Strength Groups of Common Softwoods Species

Group I	Group II
Douglas Fir Hemlock Western Larch Western Pine Southern Spruce	Cedar, Western Douglas Fir (South) Fir (White, Alpine) Hemlock (Eastern, Mountain) Pine (Eastern White, Idaho White, Lodgepole) Pine (Northern, Ponderosa, Red, Sugar, Western White) Redwood Spruce (Eastern, Engelmann)

Decking Span Chart

Maximum Allowable Span
See Dimension "A" on Page 12
Based on 1200 P.S.F. Fibre Strength Lumber – Construction Grade (No. 2) or Better.

Species Group	Laid Flat		Laid On Edge	
	1x4, 1x6, 5/4x6 (S4S, T&G, Radius Edge)	All 2x Lumber (Standard and T&G)	2x3 Lumber (Standard)	2x4 Lumber (Standard)
I	16"	60"	90"	144"
II	14"	48"	78"	120"

Joist Span Chart

Maximum Allowable Joist Span
See Dimension "B" on Page 12
Total Load 60 P.S.F. (50 P.S.F. Live Load plus 10 P.S.F. Dead Load)
Based on 1200 P.S.F. Fibre Strength Lumber – Construction Grade (No. 2) or Better.

Species Group	Joist Size	Maximum Allowable Joist Span		
		Joist Spacing 16"	24"	32"
I	2x6	9' - 6"	8' - 3"	7' - 5"
	2x8	12' - 7"	11' - 0"	10' - 0"
	2x10	16' - 1"	14' - 0"	12' - 10"
II	2x6	8' - 4"	7' - 4"	6' - 6"
	2x8	11' - 0"	9' - 8"	8' - 8"
	2x10	14' - 2"	12' - 4"	11' - 2"

Charts are Based on a 60 P.S.F. Total Load
50 P.S.F. Live Load Plus 10 P.S.F. Dead Load

Beam Spans And Post Heights

Species Group	Beam Size	Maximum Allowable Beam Spans — See Dimension "C" on Page 12 — Total Load 60 P.S.F. (50 P.S.F. Live Load plus 10 P.S.F. Dead Load) — Based on 1200 P.S.F. Fibre Strength Lumber – Construction Grade (No. 2) or Better. Beams are on edge. Span distance is center to center between posts or supports. Beam Spacing (See Dimension "B")							
		4'	**5'**	**6'**	**7'**	**8'**	**9'**	**10'**	**11'**
I	4x4	up to 4'							
	4x6	up to 6'							
	3x8	up to 8'			up to 6'				
	4x8	up to 10'	up to 9'	up to 8'	up to 7'	up to 6'			
	3x10	up to 11'	up to 10'	up to 9'	up to 8'	up to 7'	up to 6'		
	4x10	up to 12'	up to 11'	up to 10'	up to 9'	up to 8'	up to 7'		
	3x12		up to 12'	up to 11'	up to 10'	up to 9'		up to 8'	
	4x12			up to 12'		up to 11'	up to 10'	up to 9'	
	6x10					up to 12'	up to 11'	up to 10'	
	6x12						up to 12'		
II	4x4	up to 4'							
	4x6	up to 6'							
	3x8	up to 7'		up to 6'					
	4x8	up to 9'	up to 8'	up to 7'		up to 6'			
	3x10	up to 10'	up to 9'	up to 8'	up to 7'		up to 6'		
	4x10	up to 11'	up to 10'	up to 9'	up to 8'		up to 7'		up to 6'
	3x12	up to 12'	up to 11'	up to 10'	up to 9'	up to 8'		up to 7'	
	4x12		up to 12'	up to 11'	up to 10'		up to 9'	up to 8'	
	6x10			up to 12'	up to 11'	up to 10'	up to 9'		
	6x12				up to 12'		up to 11'	up to 10'	

Species Group	Beam Size	Minimum Post Heights — See Dimension "D" on Page 12 (Wood Beam Supports) — Load Area = Beam Spacing (Dim. "B") x Post Spacing (Dim. "C") in Square Feet 36 LBS.	40 LBS.	60 LBS.	72 LBS.	84 LBS.	96 LBS.	108 LBS.	120 LBS.	132 LBS.
I	4x4	up to 12' heights		up to 10' heights	up to 8' heights					
	4x6					up to 12' heights		up to 10' heights		
	6x6									up to 12' heights
II	4x4	up to 12' heights	up to 10' heights	up to 8' heights						
	4x6			up to 12' heights	up to 10' heights					
	6x6					up to 12' heights				

The deck surface is your deck's most visible element and the one that you will have to live with intimately as you use your deck. So careful planning of your deck surface is in order. If cost and ease of construction are your primary considerations, then you should stick with the classic pattern of parallel 2x6s laid perpendicular to the joists. However, if expense is not the primary consideration and you have modest construction experience, you should consider some of the other decking patterns illustrated to the right in Figures 15A-15F.

You should be aware that diagonal decking patterns require closer joist spacing to support longer decking spans when deck boards run diagonal to joists. Consequently, you must plan your deck surface in coordination with planning your deck substructure. As a rule of thumb, a complicated deck surface pattern requires a more complex and costly deck substructure.

A simpler yet visually interesting alternative to diagonal decking is to alternate widths of 2x dimensional lumber laid flat. See page 16 for patterns you can create by alternating 2x2s, 2x4s, and 2x6s.

You can design a deck surface with 2x3s or 2x4s on edge rather than laid flat. On edge decking is far more expensive than decking laid flat but can span much longer distances between joists.

The modular checkerboard pattern illustrated in Figure 15E offers bold visual impact and is not as difficult to construct as diagonal decking. However, the squares must be carefully laid out in advance so that support spacings correspond to the dimensions of the square. Extra blocking is often required so that the end of each decking board is directly supported.

Whatever deck pattern you select, space decking boards at least 3/16" for proper drainage, ventilation, and the natural shrinkage and swelling of wood.

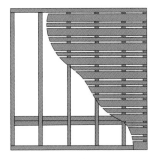

Figure 15A - Alternating 2x4s and 2x6s. This pattern provides visual interest while retaining simplicity of construction.

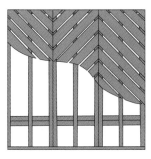

Figure 15B - Herringbone 2x6s. More difficult to construct but offers a striking visual effect.

Figure 15C - Diagonal 2x6s. Decrease joist spacing to provide additional support for diagonal decking.

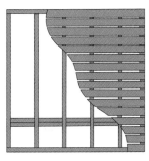

Figure 15D - Standard parallel 2x6s. This pattern is the easiest to construct of all the decking patterns.

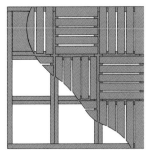

Figure 15E - Checkerboard pattern offers visual impact with relative ease of construction.

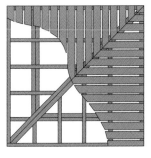

Figure 15F - L-Pattern which sets decking perpendicular to joists but requires complex deck substructure.

**Three examples of varying
the widths of decking lumber in
order to create a dramatic visual effect:**

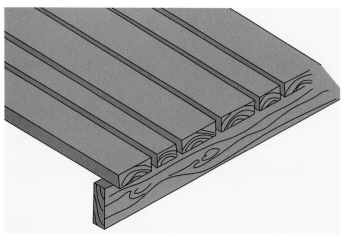

Figure 16A - 2x6 and 2x4 Wood Members

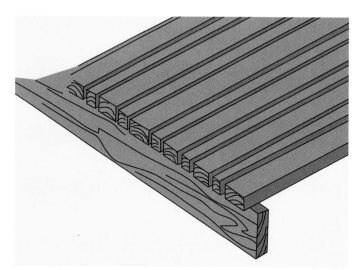

Figure 16B - 2x4 and 2x2 Wood Members

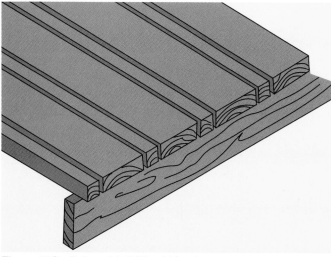

Figure 16C - 2x6 and 2x2 Wood Members

Choosing The Correct Lumber

Choosing the correct lumber for your deck can be as consequential as determining the correct design. For use in a deck, the lumber you select must perform well in an exposed outdoor environment. Performance is measured according to the following criteria:

Freedom from Shrinkage and Warping - Lumber that has dimensional stability will not cause problems later. You don't want to have to replace deck boards only 2 or 3 years after construction.

Hardness - Gives your deck durability and prevents marring of the deck surface if sharp objects are dropped.

Decay Resistance - Generally lumber cut from the heartwood (center of the log) is more resistant to decay than lumber cut from sapwood (outside of the log). However, chemical pressure-treatment can provide decay resistance to species that lack this property.

Workability - Refers to the ease with which you can saw, nail, or shape lumber.

Nail Holding - Determines whether or not a given species possesses good nail-holding power.

Paint Holding - The ability to hold a finish. Some species which contain high levels of natural extractives (such as pitch or resins) do not hold a finish well.

Fire Resistance - All woods are combustible, but some resist fire better than others. Woods that do not contain large amounts of resin are relatively slow to ignite.

Strength and Weight - Wood that is relatively light in weight but possesses great strength is ideal.

Choosing The Species Of Wood

While no single species performs ideally according to all of the criteria, your local lumber dealer will be able to advise you regarding the lumber species most suited to your area. Often you must balance considerations of economy with performance. For example, redwood is considered a premium decking material, but high transportation costs outside the area of manufacture make pressure-treated pine woods a more economical alternative. Here is a concise guide to some common softwood lumber species used in deck construction:

Cedar, Western Red - Popular for the durability and decay-resistance of its heartwood.

Cypress - Cypress resists decay, has an attractive reddish coloration, and holds paint well.

Douglas Fir, Larch - Douglas fir has great strength and is used best in the substructure of your deck, especially in the joist members.

Pines - Numerous pine species have excellent workability but must be pressure-treated for use in deck construction.

Southern Pine - Unlike the soft pines described above, southern pines possess strength but are only moderately decay and warp resistant.

Poplar - Has moderate strength, resists decay and warping.

Redwood - The premium decking material because of its durability, resistance to decay, and beautiful natural brownish-red coloration.

Spruce - Typically spruce species are readily available but do not have great decay resistance.

Remember that in certain circumstances you can use two different species of lumber to construct your deck. For example, redwood can be used for decking and post members while Douglas fir is used for strength in the deck joists and girders.

Whatever lumber species you select, study the illustrations to the right to learn the difference between the grain patterns in dimensional lumber. Flat grain lumber is cut with the grain parallel to the face of the board. Typically used for decking, flat grain boards should be used with the bark-side up in order to minimize cupping and grain separation. Vertical grain lumber, a more expensive grade used for finish work, is cut with the grain perpendicular to the face of the board.

The illustration to the right will give you an idea of some of the defects found in dimensional lumber. Typical defects are **checks** that result from separation of wood across annual rings, **knots** that result from a portion of a tree branch incorporated into cut lumber, and **splits** which are a separation of the wood due to tearing apart of wood cells. A **shake** is a lengthwise separation of the wood that usually occurs between the rings of annual growth. None of the above defects should cause you to reject lumber outright. However, wood with a **bow, cup, crook, wane, split or twist** should be avoided in deck construction.

Dimensional lumber is typically sold in incremental lengths of 8, 10, 12, 14, 16 and 20 feet. When you plan your deck, you should try to consider standard board lengths in the overall dimensions of your deck. A 12' x 16' deck (192 sq. ft.) Will be far more economical to build than a deck measuring 11' x 18' (198 sq. ft.) due to wastage.

The chart at right shows you how many decking boards to purchase for a given deck width in feet. If your deck is greater than 16 or 20 feet in length, however, you will need to purchase at least two different board lengths for every run of decking.

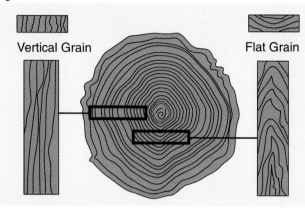

Figure 18A - Grain Location

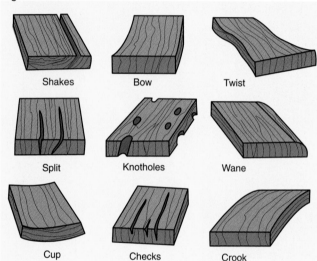

Figure 18B - Lumber Defects

Figure 18C -
Lumber Sizes

Deck Boards Required For A Given Deck Width (in feet)

Deck Width	2x4s Laid Flat	2x6s Laid Flat	2xs On Edge
8	26	16	56
9	29	18	63
10	33	21	71
11	36	23	78
12	39	25	85
13	42	27	92
14	46	29	99
15	49	31	106
16	52	33	113
17	56	35	120
18	59	37	127
19	62	39	134
20	66	42	142
21	69	44	149
22	72	46	156
23	75	48	163
24	79	50	170

Remember that the nominal dimensions of lumber do not indicate the actual finished size of dimensional lumber. For example, a 2x6 decking board measures approximately 1-1/2" x 5-1/2" depending upon moisture content and surface. Lumber that has a rough surface will measure close to the nominal size in comparison to lumber that is surfaced on four sides (known as S4S).

The most critical factor in determining actual sizes of dimensional lumber is the moisture content of the wood. Look for the grade stamp imprinted on lumber to determine moisture content. Typical moisture content ratings are:

MC 15 (less than 15% moisture content)
S-DRY (less than 19% moisture content)
S-GRN (greater than 19% moisture content)

A 2x6 surfaced unseasoned board (S-GRN) will actually measure 1-9/16" x 5-5/8" compared to 1-1/2" x 5-1/2" for a 2x6 rated surfaced dry (S-DRY). The chart at right shows actual versus nominal sizes of dimensional lumber that is S4S and S-DRY or better.

It is wise to avoid unseasoned lumber especially in the selection of your decking. Decking which is unseasoned can shrink considerably as it dries naturally and will leave hazardous gaps over 1/4" between deck boards.

Standard Dimensions of Surfaced Lumber	
Nominal Size	Surfaced (Actual) Size
1 x 2	3/4" x 1-1/2"
1 x 3	3/4" x 2-1/2"
1 x 4	3/4" x 3-1/2"
1 x 6	3/4" x 5-1/2"
1 x 8	3/4" x 7-1/4"
1 x 10	3/4" x 9-1/4"
1 x 12	3/4" x 11-1/4"
2 x 3	1-1/2" x 2-1/2"
2 x 4	1-1/2" x 3-1/2"
2 x 6	1-1/2" x 5-1/2"
2 x 8	1-1/2" x 7-1/4"
2 x 10	1-1/2" x 9-1/4"
2 x 12	1-1/2" x 11-1/4"
4 x 4	3-1/2" x 3-1/2"
4 x 10	3-1/2" x 9-1/4"
6 x 8	5-1/2" x 7-1/2"

ORDERING DECK MATERIALS

Complete the sample material list on page 20 before you begin to shop. If you are using one of the pre-drawn deck plans offered in the back of this manual, each plan comes with a complete list of materials. If you have designed your own deck, create a material list from the final design after approval by your local building department.

Once you have completed the sample material list, visit Menards Building Materials Desk to shop for your materials. Be aware that you will add to the cost of your project if you purchase your materials in a piecemeal fashion. Keep in mind that Menards offers quality materials and the level of service provided to make your deck building project easier.

Especially consider the quality and grade of the lumber you are purchasing. Poor quality materials will yield a meager return on your deck investment. Finally, if you are a novice Do-It-Yourselfer, don't forget that a dealer who provides knowledgeable service as well as economical materials can save you from costly and time-consuming errors.

Don't hesitate to order at least a 5-10% overage of materials to make up for inevitable cutting mistakes or lumber defects. Be aware that dimensional lumber is sold either by the board foot, the lineal (or running) foot, or by the piece. A board foot of lumber represents the amount of lumber in a board 1" thick x 12" wide x 12" long. Use the following formula to compute board feet:

$$\text{Board Feet} = \frac{\text{Length (Feet)} \times \text{Width (Inches)} \times \text{Thickness (Inches)}}{12}$$

SAMPLE MATERIALS LIST

	Size	Length	Quantity	X	Cost	=	Total Cost
Foundation							
Concrete							
Sand							
Gravel							
Substructure							
Posts							
Girders							
Deck Joists							
Rim Joists							
Ledger							
Bracing							
Fascia/Trim Boards							
Miscellaneous							
Surface Lumber							
Decking							
Stairs							
Stair Stringer							
Stair Riser							
Stair Tread							
Railings							
Railings							
Balusters							
Connectors							
Nails							
Joist Hangers							
Joist Anchors							
Post Base Anchors							
Post Caps							
Lag Bolts w/ Washers							
Screws							
Grand Total							

NAILS AND FASTENERS

Nails are the most common fastener used in deck framing and construction. Nail lengths are indicated by the term penny, noted by a small letter **d**. In most cases, nails increase in diameter as they increase in length. Heavier construction framing is accomplished with common nails. The extra thick shank of the common nail has greater strength than other types. A wide thick head spreads the load and resists pull-through. For the substructure of your deck where nails are hidden, consider vinyl coated sinkers or cement coated nails which bond to the wood and will not pull up as readily as uncoated nails.

To fasten your decking planks to deck joists, use hot-dipped galvanized common nails, typically 10d or longer. To prevent splitting, predrill nail holes through decking. Spiral nails or annular ring nails provide greater holding power and are less likely to pull up with weathering of your deck. If you have selected redwood for decking, avoid poor-quality nails that will react with the decay-resisting substances in the wood and cause unsightly stains. Finally, consider deck screws as the most expensive but most flexible means of fastening your decking. Deck screws will not pull out and easily allow replacement of individual deck boards at a later time.

Box nails are similar in shape to common nails, but they have a slimmer shank that is less likely to split wood. Finishing nails are used in work where you want to counter sink and then cover the nail head.

Screws create neat, strong joints for finished work. Heavy-duty lag screws and lag bolts are useful for heavier framing connections, such as girder-to-post.

Discuss your project with your local Menards Building Materials Desk associate to determine the best nail and fastener selections for your deck project.

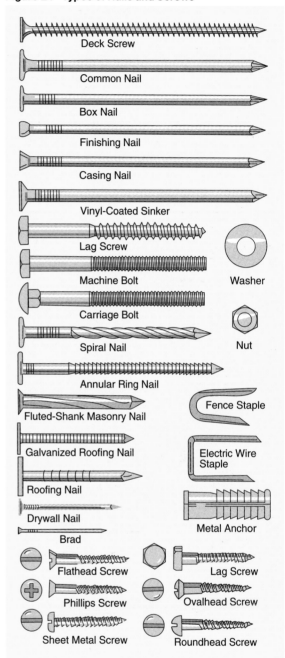

Figure 21 - Types of Nails and Screws

Table of Common Nails

Size	Length	Gauge	# per lb.
2d	1"	15	840
3d	1 1/4"	14	540
4d	1 1/2"	12 1/2	290
5d	1 3/4"	12 1/2	250
6d	2"	11 1/2	160
7d	2 1/4"	11 1/2	150
8d	2 1/2"	10 1/4	100
9d	2 3/4"	10 1/4	90
10d	3"	9	65
12d	3 1/4"	9	60
16d	3 1/2"	8	45
20d	4"	6	30
30d	4 1/2"	5	20
40d	5"	4	16
50d	5 1/2"	3	12
60d	6"	2	10

Finishing Nail Selection Chart

Size	Length	Gauge	# per lb.
2d	1"	16	1000
3d	1 1/4"	15 1/2	870
4d	1 1/2"	15	600
6d	2"	13	310
8d	2 1/2"	12 1/2	190
10d	3"	11 1/2	120

These tables show the approximate number of nails you get in a pound. You'll need more pounds of larger sizes to do a job. For outside jobs, get galvanized or cadmium-plated nails. Aluminum nails are a bit more expensive unless you are doing a smaller project.

Screw Selection Chart

Size	Length	Size	Length
0	1/4-3/8	9	1/2-3
1	1/4-1/2	10	1/2-3 1/2
2	1/4-3/4	11	5/8-3 1/2
3	1/4-1	12	5/8-4
4	1/4-1 1/2	14	3/4-5
5	3/8-1 1/2	16	1-5
6	3/8-2 1/2	18	1 1/4-5
7	3/8-2 1/2	20	1 1/2-5
8	3/8-3	24	3-5

The screw chart shows sizes and the lengths in which they're available. The larger sizes come in longer lengths. Most jobs call for sizes 6-12 in 1/2 to 3 inch lengths. Check size and length before you buy.

A wide variety of metal fasteners are available to make your deck sturdy and long-lasting. You may be required by local codes to add seismic/hurricane connectors to each joist where it connects to the supporting girder. Post cap connectors and the anchor base connectors illustrated below are a superior means of fastening compared to toenailing. Be certain that connectors are level and square before you secure the post with nails at the nailing holes in the metal connector. Follow the manufacturer's installation instructions.

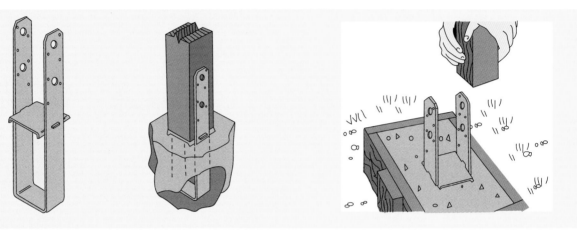

Figure 22A - Post Base Anchor
Available sizes for: 4x4 Posts, 4x6 Posts, 6x6 Posts

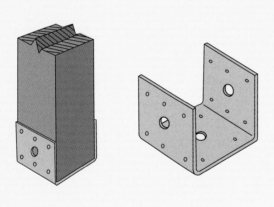

Figure 22B - Post Anchor
Available sizes for: 4x and 6x Posts

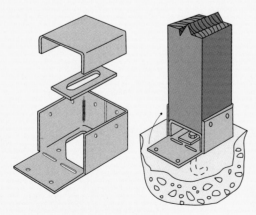

Figure 22C - Adjustable Post Anchor
Available sizes for: 4x4 Posts, 4x6 Posts, 6x6 Posts

Right-angled corner framing anchors add strength to perpendicular butt joints, especially where rim joists meet. Use joist hangers to attach your deck joists to rim joist members. The modest additional expense of metal fasteners will be more than offset by the added durability of your deck. Remember that metal fasteners help your deck to withstand the expansion and contraction of wood that occurs with changes of season. Secure fasteners using the short ribbed nails provided or where extra strength is required use lag screws in addition to nails.

Figure 23A - Post Base
Available sizes for: **4x4 Posts, 4x6 Posts, 6x6 Posts**

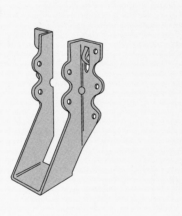

Figure 23B - Joist Hangers
Available sizes for: **2x4, 2x6, 2x8, 2x10, and 2x12 Joists**

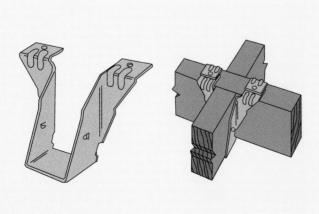

Figure 23C - Beam Frame Connector
Available sizes for: **2x4 Joists and 2x6 Joists**

Generic Step-By-Step Instructions For Building A Low-Level Attached Deck

1. Site Preparation

Obtain a building permit if required and ensure that you will not be building your deck on top of sewer, gas, or electrical lines that require service. Grade your site and install drainage if necessary.

2. Laying Out the Deck

Mark the position of the deck on your house wall following the deck framing plan. Measure out from the house the depth of your deck and drive a stake to mark each corner. Construct batterboards two feet each way past the outer corners using 2x4 stakes. The top of the batterboards must be level. Extend string lines across the batterboards to outline the deck. Place additional stakes for string lines to locate the top of concrete piers. Each string line should be taut and level. Your outline can also be squared by measuring along one side a distance of 4 feet. Your outline will be square when the diagonal dimension between the two points measures 5 feet. Repeat the process at the opposite corner.

3. Locating Deck Piers

Following the deck framing plan, locate the piers. Place a wood stake in the ground to mark the center of each pier. The string lines you placed above will help you to determine the correct top height for each pier.

4. Determining Height of Deck

In order to determine the height of your deck you must first determine the height of your house floor from your grade line. Once you have determined this height, allow for a 2" to 4" step down from your house floor to the deck so that water will not enter the house. The remaining dimension will be the height of your post from the bottom of the girder to grade line.

5. Attaching the Ledger

Cut ledger to size and brace against the house wall at desired height. Level the ledger with a carpenter's level. Temporarily nail the ledger in place at opposite ends and then recheck for levelness. Once ledger is level, secure to house with 3/8" lag screws that are at least 2" longer than the thickness of the ledger. Use a washer on each fastener and space at 24" maximum intervals.

6. Installing Piers and Posts

Dig pier holes 12" in diameter to the necessary depth required by your area. The depth of the hole should be at least half the height of the 4x4 post above ground. Some local codes require that your pier hole extend at least 6 inches below the local frost line. If you are using precast concrete piers, fill the hole with sufficient concrete to embed the pier at least 4" in the concrete and set the pier square and level in its footing. Use the string line to adjust the pier to the correct height. Fasten post base anchor to nailer block on pier.

If you are creating your own pier, build pier forms then fill the hole with concrete. When concrete first starts to set, position a post base anchor in each pier and make sure the post base is centered and level. Begin to secure 4x4 posts by starting with the lower level post closest to the house. This post will serve as the base post for setting the heights of all other posts. Tie a string line to a nail set flush with the top of the ledger board. Extend the other end of the string over the top of the base post and attach a line level and mark each post at proper height. Cut off excess post. Plumb and square post with a level. Nail posts to post base anchors.

7. Installing the Girders

Cut the girders to their proper lengths following the deck framing plan. Square up corners of girders and be sure all outer edges are in line. Secure girders to posts with post cap connectors.

8. Attaching Joists and Rim Joists

Cut the rim joists to their proper lengths. Attach metal joist hangers to ledger board at 16" or 24" intervals and to opposite rim joist at proper interval. Make certain hangers are square and at proper height. Set the first joist in first hanger on the ledger board. This joist should be level on the top of the girders if you have planned correctly. Install remaining joists in their hangers. Set the rim joist opposite the ledger in place and secure by fastening joists to joist hangers. Secure two additional rim joists to ledger board and opposite rim joist with corner framing anchors. Ensure that all rim joists are square and that deck joists are straight in hangers. Nail deck joists to hangers and use joist ties to fasten joists to girders.

9. Nailing the Decking

Start with the first board along the house wall and allow a 3/8" expansion joint between first board and the wall. Since this first board will serve as a guide for the rest of the decking, place it as square as possible. To prevent against splitting, pre-drill slightly undersized pilot holes at each location where you will fasten decking to the joist. Use three 12 penny hot-dipped galvanized nails at the end of each board and two nails at the joists. Snap a chalk line to keep your nails in a straight line. Use 16 penny nails as spacers for a 3/16" gap between deck boards. When 6 feet of decking remains to be placed, adjust board spacing to avoid a gap at the end of the deck. When all the decking is in place, snap a chalk line along the outside face of the end joists. Cut the deck boards at the chalk line so they're flush with rim joists. Set trim boards flush with decking top and nail to rim joists.

10. Finishing

If you so desire, apply a paint or stain to your finished deck in accordance with manufacturer's instructions provided with the product.

Check and recheck your foundation pier layout plan. Errors at this stage are costly and difficult to correct. You must layout the deck and locate piers with accuracy.

Be certain that you know the location of all underground utility and septic lines that may interfere with construction of your deck. Do NOT locate your deck over or near an active septic tank.

Mark the position of your ledger board on your house wall following the deck framing plan. You can either install the ledger (see pages 28-29) temporarily at this time or pencil mark the location and install the ledger later.

Measure out from the house the depth of your deck and drive a stake to mark each corner. Construct batterboards 24" each way past the outer corners using 2x4 stakes as shown below. Drive the stakes holding the batterboards securely into the ground. Use your carpenter's level and a straight 2x4 or a string level on a nylon string to ensure that the tops of the batterboards are level and at the same height as the top of your ledger.

Extend nylon string lines across the batterboards to outline the deck. Each perimeter string should be taut and level. It helps to cut a notch at the top of the batterboard to hold the string line securely in place.

To ensure squareness form a 3-4-5 right triangle with the string lines. Using a felt tipped pen, mark the string line 4 feet out from where the lines intersect. Then mark the other line 3 feet out from the crossing point. Finally measure the distance diagonally between the marks on both string lines. When the distance measures exactly five feet your deck outline is square. Remember that the system of the 3-4-5 right triangle works in any multiple of 3-4-5 such as 6-8-10 or 9-12-15. Repeat this process at each corner of the deck.

Check that your work is square by measuring diagonally from opposite corner marks in an X formation. If your diagonal measurements are equal, your deck perimeter layout is aligned properly. If the measurements are not equal, recheck your work and adjust string lines until they are correct.

Next determine the location for each pier following the deck foundation pier layout plan. Measure along opposite perimeter strings and mark the points that represent the pier centerline(s). Place a stake at these marks and then attach a level string to show the centerline of the piers. This string should be at the same height as the perimeter strings. Mark the location of each pier on the pier centerline string and drop a plumb bob to mark the center of each pier. Identify the center of each pier location with a stake. Place a string for each row of piers.

Figure 26 - Marking Corner Stakes

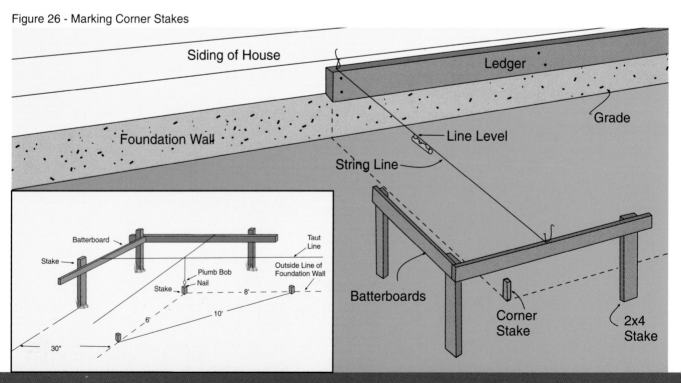

Dig pier holes 10"-12" in diameter. It's best to move the string lines temporarily before you dig. Depth of pier holes depends upon your local building codes and the level of your local frost line. Use a shovel or post hole digger to dig holes with straight rather than sloping sides. Dig the hole deep enough to allow for 4" of compacted gravel at the bottom of the hole.

Tap the soil at the bottom of the hole to prevent settling of the pier. Add approximately 4" of gravel to the bottom of the hole. At this point you can add reinforcing bar if your local codes require it. The reinforcing bar adds strength to deep concrete piers. The completed hole should be deep enough to allow the top of the completed pier to sit approximately 4"- 6" inches above the finished grade line. Replace string lines and recheck your work.

Figure 27 - Digging Pier Holes

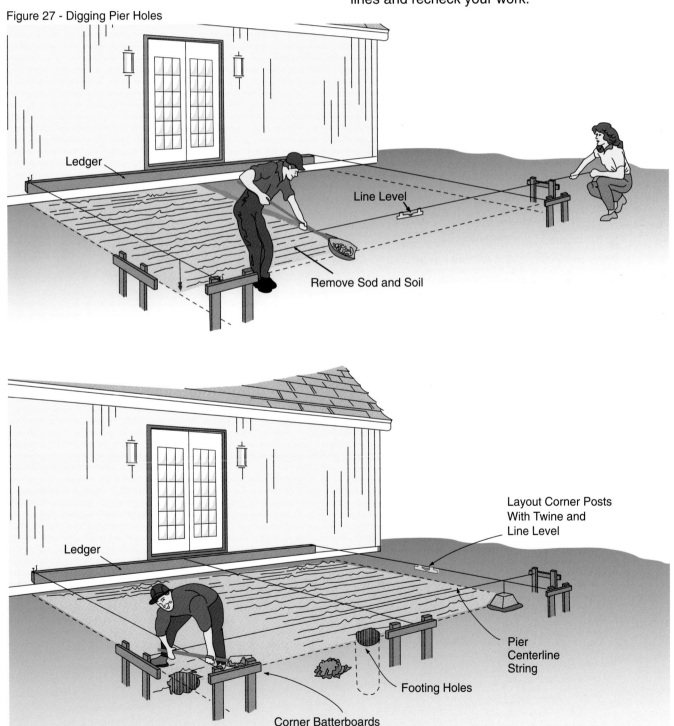

Ledger

Line Level

Remove Sod and Soil

Ledger

Layout Corner Posts With Twine and Line Level

Pier Centerline String

Footing Holes

Corner Batterboards

Study the illustrations below and on page 29 which demonstrate different methods of attaching a ledger board to the outside wall of your home.

1. Select only a straight board which is either pressure-treated or cut from a decay resistant species such as redwood or cedar for your ledger. You don't want the ledger to warp or decay and cause severe problems at a later date.

2. Position the ledger so that you step down from the house onto the deck. If the ledger board is higher than your house floor, water can run into the house from the deck. Remember that you will apply decking on top of the ledger and joist subsystem when you determine the height of the ledger in relation to the house floor.

3. Be sure to locate and reroute if necessary all utility lines which might run in the wall where you will attach the ledger.

4. Brace the ledger against the house wall at the desired height.

5. Mark holes for lag bolts or screws on the ledger board. Typically the holes occur in pairs, one on top of the other, at the end of the ledger and then alternate in an up and down pattern. See Figure 29A. Be careful not to place your holes where you will affix joist hangers.

6. Use rustproof hot-dipped galvanized lag screws or bolts. If you are fastening the ledger to aluminum siding, use aluminum screws and washers to prevent corrosion.

7. You might want to paint the exposed cut ends of the ledger with a preservative to prevent decay.

For **wood walls**, temporarily nail once at the board's approximate center, level the board with a carpenter's level, and temporarily nail both ends. Recheck for levelness. If the ledger is level, fasten to the wall with lag screws and washers. To prevent trapping of moisture between the ledger and the exterior wall, you might want to place two or three washers over the lag screw on the back (house) side of the ledger to act as spacers.

For **stucco walls**, first drill lag screw holes into the ledger with a wood bit. Then use makeshift braces for support or enlist extra helping hands to hold the ledger in position and mark the stucco through the ledger holes with a pencil. Be certain that the ledger is level before you mark the holes on the stucco. These marked holes must be drilled with a masonry bit in order to penetrate the stucco. Once you have drilled through the stucco, you can again switch to a wood bit and then drill a slightly undersized hole (for example use a 1/4" bit for 3/8" lag screws) into the house floor frame header board.

For **masonry walls**, drill lag screw holes into the ledger with a wood bit. Then use makeshift braces for support or enlist extra helping hands to hold the ledger in position and mark the masonry through the ledger holes with a pencil. Be certain that the ledger is level before you mark the holes on the masonry. Drill with a masonry bit and create a hole wide and deep enough to accommodate an expansion shield for the lag bolt. Carefully seat the expansion shield, place the ledger board against the wall, and secure with lag bolts and washers.

Figure 28A - Attaching to Masonry

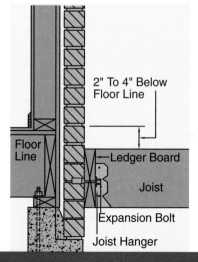

Figure 28B - Attaching to Wood

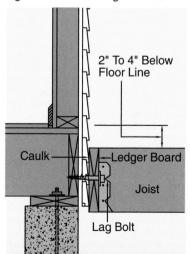

Figure 28C - Bolting Ledger to House

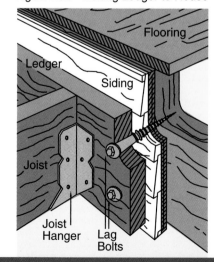

Figure 29A - Attaching Ledger Board

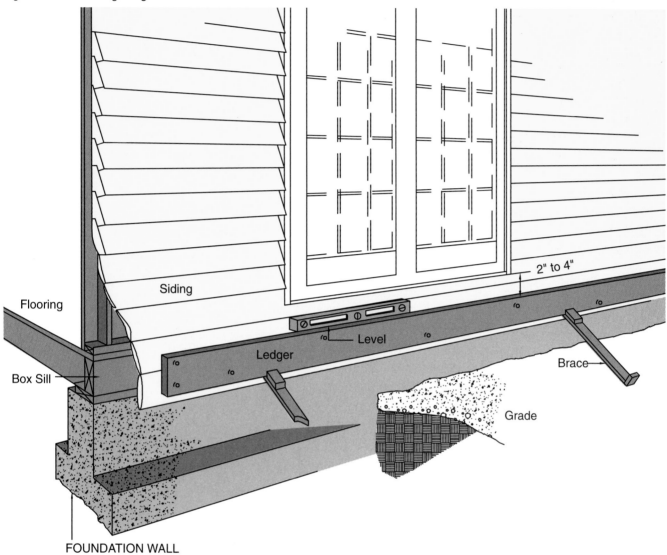

Figure 29B - Ledger Board Detail

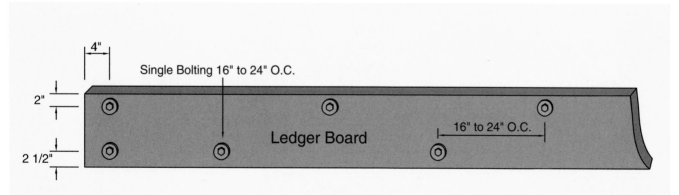

First be certain you have purchased enough concrete to complete pier installation. Concrete is measured in cubic yards. To calculate the concrete required for a given number of cylindrical piers, use the following formula to find the **Total Volume in cubic yards:**

$$\textbf{Volume} = \frac{3.14 \times \text{Depth of Pier (feet)} \times \text{Diameter (feet)} \times \text{Diameter (feet)} \times \text{No. Piers}}{108}$$

Example: Concrete required for twelve 10" diameter piers, 30" deep.*

$$\textbf{Volume in cubic yards} = \frac{3.14 \times 2.5 \times .83 \times .83 \times 12}{108} = \textbf{.61 Cubic Yards}$$

*Remember to convert inches to feet (10 inches = .83 feet)   Conversion Factor: 27 Cubic Feet = 1 Cubic Yard

Figure 30A - Pier Diagrams

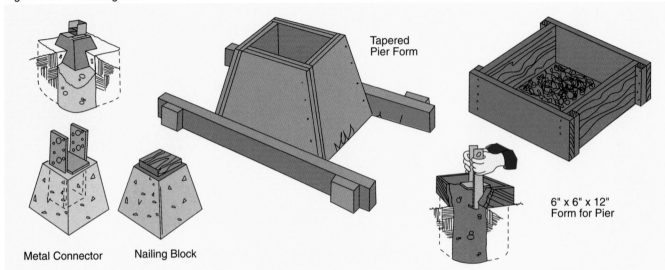

Tapered Pier Form

Metal Connector   Nailing Block

6" x 6" x 12" Form for Pier

Figure 30B - Pillars and Posts

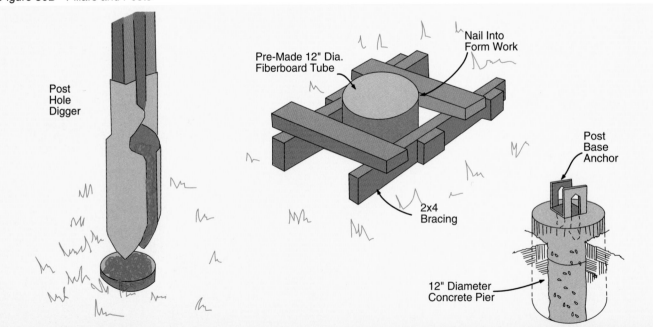

Post Hole Digger

Pre-Made 12" Dia. Fiberboard Tube

Nail Into Form Work

2x4 Bracing

Post Base Anchor

12" Diameter Concrete Pier

Prepare pier forms if you are going to make poured in-place piers. Otherwise obtain precast piers with a redwood or pressure treated nailer block on top. You might want to temporarily remove pier centerline strings at this point.

1. Mix concrete according to manufacturer's instructions in a wheelbarrow or in a "half-bag" mixer. Use clean water for mixing and achieve the proper plastic consistency before you pour the concrete. If you are not using ready-mix concrete, prepare a **1:2:3 mix**–one part concrete, two parts river sand, and three parts gravel.

2. Coat the inside of the forms with oil to prevent sticking and dampen the inside of the hole with water before you pour the concrete.

3. With your post base anchors at hand, poor the concrete into the forms and tap slightly to settle. For poured in-place piers, wait for the concrete to begin to harden and set the post base anchors into the concrete. Ensure that anchors are square and level. You can drop a plumb bob from your centerline string to be certain that your anchor is centered properly. Adjust post base anchors to the correct height.

4. If you are using a precast pier, fill the pier hole with concrete up to 2"- 3" below grade level. Then spray the pier with water and then embed the pier at least 3" into the fresh concrete and twist slightly to achieve a solid bond between the concrete and the pier. Make certain that you have enough concrete in the hole so that the top of the nailer block is at least 4"- 6" above grade level. Check the alignment of the pier by dropping the plumb bob from the centerline string. Finally, use a level across the nailer block and tap the pier until it is level in all directions and square.

5. Allow the concrete to harden at least 24 hours before you proceed to attach posts to piers. If you have poured your concrete during hot and dry conditions, you should cover the piers with wet burlap sacks to encourage a slow cure of the concrete.

6. If you are using precast piers and decide to secure post anchor connectors to the nailer block, wait for concrete to harden and then nail the post anchors to the nailer block with short ribbed nails.

Figure 31 - Installation and Base Anchor Techniques

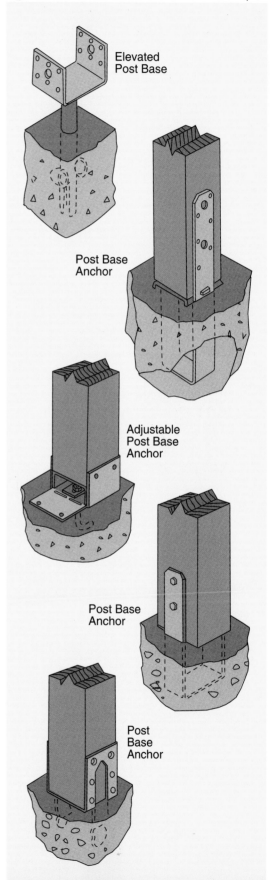

Elevated Post Base

Post Base Anchor

Adjustable Post Base Anchor

Post Base Anchor

Post Base Anchor

If you are building railings, some posts will extend above the deck floor to provide railing support. Follow the post bracing instructions for high-level decks but do not cut posts at the girder line.

1. Cut deck posts individually to at least 6" longer than finished post height. If you are uncertain as to the approximate finished height, drop your plumb bob from the pier centerline string and measure the distance from the string (which should be at the height of the top of the girder) to the bottom seat of post anchor connector or to the top of the nailing block. First subtract the actual height (remember that a 4x6 girder for example is only 5-1/2" high) of the girder and then add 6" to this distance to calculate your rough-in post height.

2. If your deck is a low-level deck with short posts (under 12"), simply seat the rough-in posts in the post anchor connectors, check for plumb with a level, and ensure that posts are square in the connector. Use either the pier centerline string to establish a cutting line on the post or use a string level on a line from the top of the ledger board to the post. Again you must subtract the actual (versus nominal) height of the girder from your string line to establish the cutting line on the post.

3. If your deck is a high-level deck with posts over 12", use the following instructions to ensure that posts are plumb and cut at the correct height for the girder.

4. Follow the illustration to the right and use scrap lumber to stake and support the post. First use a carpenter's level on two adjacent sides of the post to ensure that the post is plumb and then use a string level to determine the correct height of the post in relation to the ledger board. Remember that you must subtract the actual height of the girder from your stringline to establish your cutting line. Mark the cutting line with a pencil.

5. Cut marked posts at the post cutting line. Be certain that your cut through the post is a level cut.

6. Recheck your posts for plumb and either toenail (driving the nails at an angle on all four sides) the post to the pier's nailing block or seat the post in the post anchor and use short ribbed nails provided with the connector or at least 10 penny common HDG nails to connect the post to the post anchor. Nail at all the nailing holes provided in the post anchor. In earthquake prone regions, you can use lag screws to connect the post and the anchor for extra security.

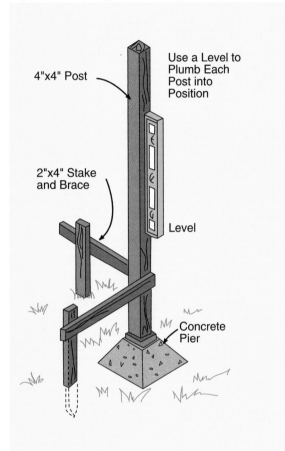

Figure 32A - Setting and Plumbing Posts

4"x4" Post

Use a Level to Plumb Each Post into Position

2"x4" Stake and Brace

Level

Concrete Pier

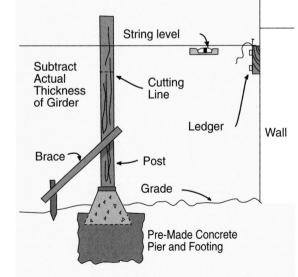

Figure 32B - Measuring Deck Post Height

String level

Subtract Actual Thickness of Girder

Cutting Line

Ledger

Wall

Brace

Post

Grade

Pre-Made Concrete Pier and Footing

INSTALLING THE GIRDERS

Girders can be either solid or built-up from two or more 2x boards on edge. Remember that because of extra thickness 4x beams will support a greater load than built-up 2x beams. Also a 4x6 girder for example sits squarely on top of a 4x4 post (both are 3 1/2" wide) while two 2x6s spliced together (2 x 1-1/2" = 3") do not make an even connection. Whatever type of girder you select, make certain that girders are true and not badly bowed.

You might need some extra hands to lift a heavy girder into place. Use shims between girder and posts where necessary to correct for short post height and level girder before fastening to post. For the best joining of girder to post, use post cap connectors (see illustrations below for various girder to post connector options). Otherwise you can toenail girders to posts with 16 or 20 penny HDG common nails.

Figure 33 - Girder Connectors

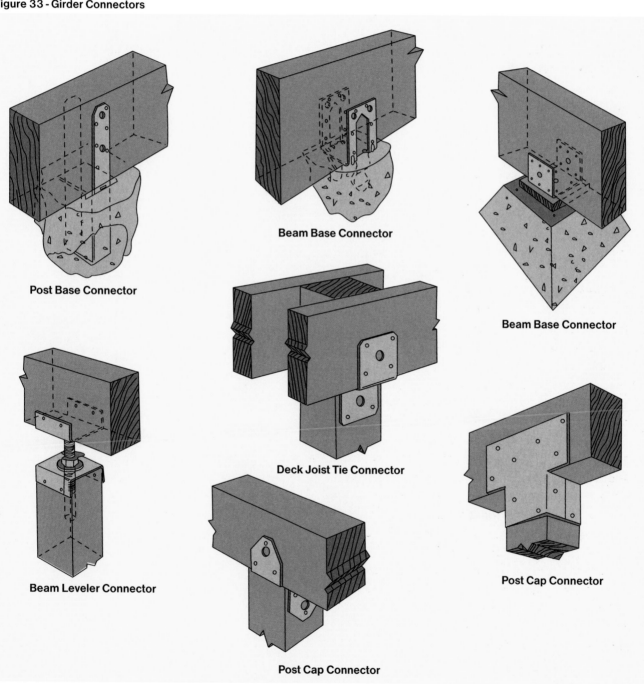

Post Base Connector

Beam Base Connector

Beam Base Connector

Beam Leveler Connector

Deck Joist Tie Connector

Post Cap Connector

Post Cap Connector

1. First place rim joists (also known as perimeter or band joists) on edge at ends of ledger. Locate the joists so that the bow side of the board is facing up. Next attach rim joist to ledger with corner framing anchors or toenail to ledger board with 12 penny common nails. Be certain that rim joists run at a true right angle to your ledger.

2. Place the rim joist opposite the ledger board and use corner anchors and nails to secure the connection. Make sure that all rim joists and ledger meet at right angles and realign them if they do not.

3. Depending on the joist spacing indicated on your deck framing plan, mark the center location of joist hangers on both the ledger and the opposite rim joist. Affix joist hangers with short ribbed nails provided in accordance with the manufacturer's instructions.

4. Measure each joist individually and cut to size. Set the first joist in its hangers on the ledger board and opposite rim joist. This joist should be level on the top of the girders if you have planned correctly. Making sure that the joist is level and perpendicular, nail to both joist hangers. Follow this procedure until all joists are installed.

5. If you are using 2x8 or larger joists, you should consider installing cross blocking boards or metal cross bracing at mid-span to keep joists from flexing over spans greater than 8 feet.

6. Use **seismic/hurricane connectors** (also known as joist anchors) illustrated at the bottom of page 35 (see Figure 35C) to secure each joist as it crosses a girder. Otherwise toenail joist to beam with common nails on both sides of the joist.

Figure 34 - Basic Deck Components

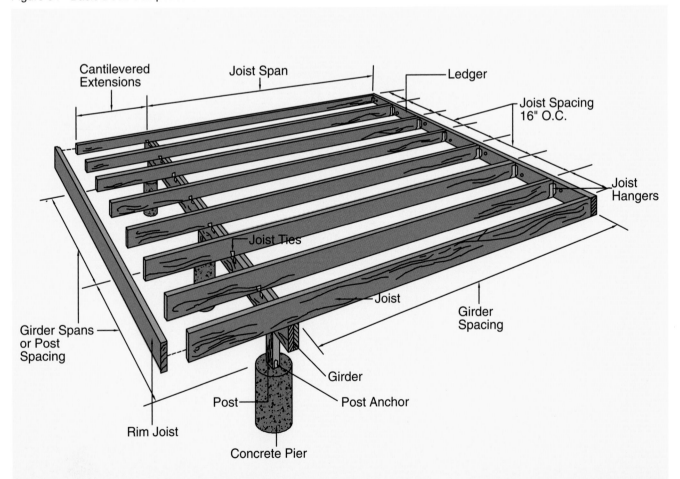

Figure 35A - Joist Hanger

Figure 35B - Beam Frame Connector

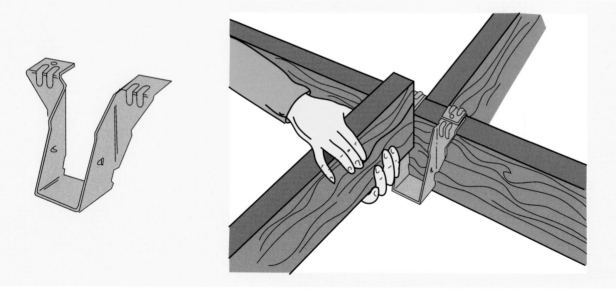

Figure 35C - Seismic/Hurricane Anchor

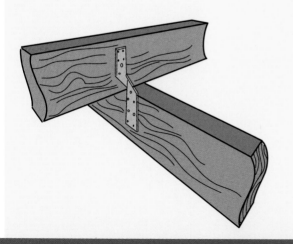

Figure 35D - Twist Strap Metal Connectors

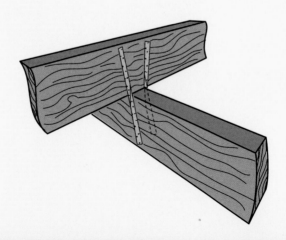

Consult your local building codes for post bracing requirements for high decks. Additional factors which require post bracing are high winds, unusual deck loads like a portable spa placed on the deck surface, or earthquake activity.

Use 2x4s to brace distance less than 8 feet and 2x6s for distances greater than 8 feet.

Use at least four 3/8" x 3" lag screws and washers (two at each connection point) when you attach the brace to the post.

If you are using the **X-brace** shown at right, drill a hole where the braces intersect and secure the braces with one 3/8" x 3-1/2" lag bolt and washer.

If you construct the **Y-brace** shown below, leave approximately 1/4" gap between the two braces where they come together to ensure proper drainage. The angle where your braces meet on the post should not exceed 90 degrees.

Always cut your braces on the diagonal and cover the entire width of the post to which the brace is connected. Square cut braces detract from the appearance of your deck.

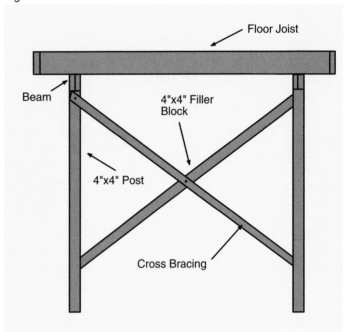

Figure 36A - X-Brace

Floor Joist
Beam
4"x4" Filler Block
4"x4" Post
Cross Bracing

Figure 36B - Y-Brace

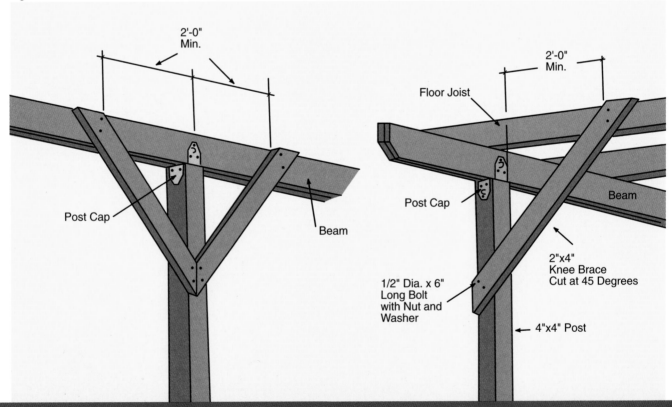

2'-0" Min.
Post Cap
Beam

2'-0" Min.
Floor Joist
Post Cap
Beam
1/2" Dia. x 6" Long Bolt with Nut and Washer
2"x4" Knee Brace Cut at 45 Degrees
4"x4" Post

STAIR CONSTRUCTION

A solid concrete stair pad is the key to successful stair construction. Don't attempt to anchor your stairs directly into the ground. Add stairs before you place surface decking.

When you have more than three steps up to your deck, you should construct a hand rail on each side of the stairs. Consult your local building code requirements.

Two stair construction methods are illustrated below-using cut stringers (upper) or the stair support method (lower). Instructions for cutting stringers are provided on page 38. The following instructions utilize the stair support method that is easier for the novice builder.

Measure the vertical height (rise) from grade to top of decking. For a 7" stair rise, divide rise dimension by 7" that will tell you how many stair risers are required. You will need two 10-1/4" metal stair supports for each stair and two 2x6 stair treads cut to a minimum 36" stair width.

Cut 2x10 or 2x12 stair stringers to size and fasten to the deck framing with a 3" corner angles and 1/4" x 1-1/2" lag screws. Use a masonry bit to drill holes for expansion shields into stair pad. Use lag screws to connect bottom corner angles to stringers and measure stringers to ensure they are parallel at top and bottom. Bolt bottom corner angles to expansion shields. Mark the step support positions on both stringers with the support below the stair tread. Use 1/4" x 1-1/2" lag screws to fasten 10-1/4" step supports to stringers and to install 2x6 stair treads.

Figure 37A - Stringers

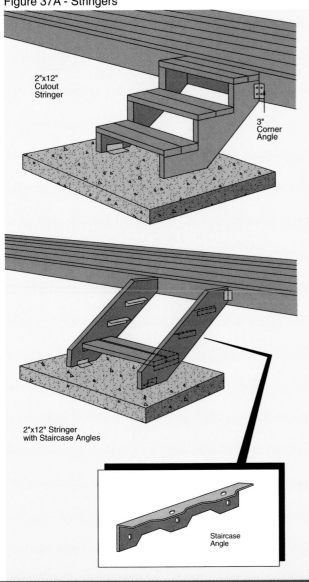

2"x12" Cutout Stringer

3" Corner Angle

2"x12" Stringer with Staircase Angles

Staircase Angle

Figure 37B - Risers

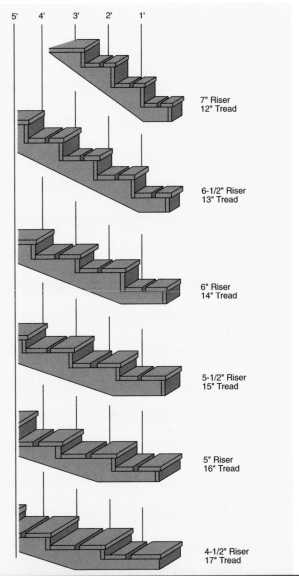

5' 4' 3' 2' 1'

7" Riser
12" Tread

6-1/2" Riser
13" Tread

6" Riser
14" Tread

5-1/2" Riser
15" Tread

5" Riser
16" Tread

4-1/2" Riser
17" Tread

If you attempt to cut your own stair stringers rather than use metal stair supports, you must select solid 2x12 material free from knots and other defects for your stringers. A stair stringer cutting template is available to help you cut stringers.

Stringer Instructions:

1. Measure the distance from the top of the deck to the grade in inches. Divide distance by 7.25". Round off the solution to the next higher whole number. Divide the distance from the top of the porch to the grade by this whole number. The solution to the step you just completed will be your riser height.

2. Place a carpenter's square on a 2x12 as shown on page 39. Locate the 10-3/4" mark on the outside of the square's long leg. Place this mark on an edge of the 2x12. While holding this point in place, rotate the square until you can read your riser dimension on the outside edge of the short leg. Line the riser dimension up with the edge of the 2x12. Draw a line along both outside edges of the square. This marking constitutes one square and riser.

3. Slide the square along the 2x12 until you can align the 10-3/4" mark with the intersections of the edge of the board and the top of the first riser you marked. Again while holding this point in place, rotate the square until you can read your riser dimension on the outside edge of the short leg. Line the riser dimension up with the edge of the 2x12. Draw lines along both outside edges of the square. This mark outlines the second tread and riser. Repeat this process until you have drawn the required number of risers for your site condition.

4. Once all the treads and risers have been marked, move down to the line at the base of the first riser and extend that line across the 2x12. Measure 3-1/2" up from this line and draw a parallel line. This line is the actual bottom of the stringer.

Note: This 3-1/2" is a constant regardless of what you have calculated your particular riser height to be. The 3-1/2" is made up from the 1-1/2" thickness of the first tread and the 2" thickness of the concrete that is above grade.

5. Next extend the line formed by the top tread. Measure along this line 3-1/2" past the line of the top riser to locate the back of the stringer. Draw a line from this point, perpendicular to the tread, and extend to underside of stringer.

6. To lay out the notch in the underside of the stringer extend the line of the top riser to the underside of the stringer. Measure over 1-1/2" and draw a parallel line. Now take the carpenter's square and place the 1-1/2" mark from the outside edge of the square's long leg on the point where the line of the top riser intersects the underside of the stringer. Rotate the long leg of the square until it is parallel with the treads. When it is parallel, the short leg of the square will fall along the line measured 1-1/2" over from the line of the top riser. Connect the two lines with a perpendicular line drawn along the outside edge of the square's long leg.

7. Cut out the stringer on the lines that form the treads and risers, the bottom of the stringer, the back of the stringer, and the notch in the underside. Use your power saw carefully and cut each line exactly. Check the stringer by putting it in place on the rim joist and concrete pad. When one stringer has been cut correctly, you can use it as a template for the other two stringers. Again be certain that you do not cut stringers beyond the marked lines.

8. Measure for proper width between stringers at deck attachment point and attach stringers to the deck by using either a corner anchor or joist hanger. Then measure stringers at pad for proper width and mark holes for expansion shields in concrete. Drill holes with a masonry bit. Affix 5" corner anchor to concrete pad and to stringers using 1/4" x 1-1/2" lag screws and washers. Nail each stair tread with bark side up to the stringer with 12 penny hot-dipped galvanized nails or use at least 3" deck screws. You might want to predrill nail holes to prevent splitting of the stair treads.

Two Stair Support Methods

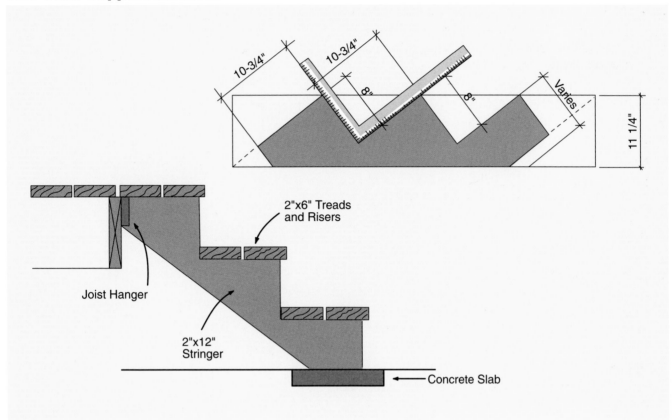

Figure 39A - Steps with Notched Stringers

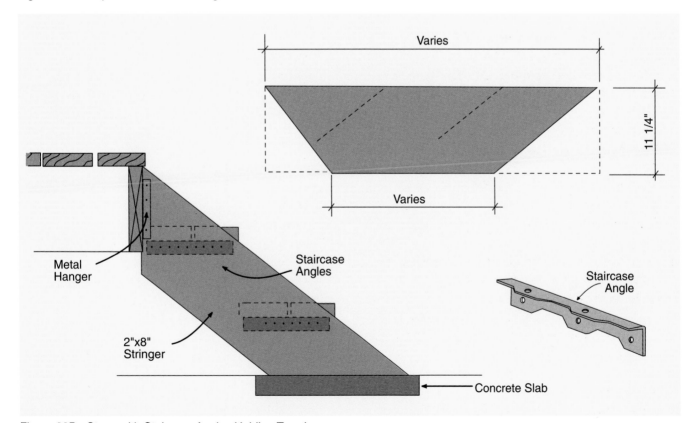

Figure 39B - Steps with Staircase Angles Holding Treads

Installing decking boards provides great satisfaction as your deck nears completion. However, since the decking is the most visible part of your deck, you must proceed carefully as you nail the decking in place.

Select decking boards that are straight and free from defects. If you try to use severely warped or bowed lumber, your installation process will be tedious and you will be unhappy with the finished result.

The following instructions are for parallel decking boards laid flat and installed perpendicular to deck joists. If you are installing your decking on the diagonal, these exact instructions do not apply but the methods are similar. For diagonal decking you still start from one edge and work out from that edge until all decking is in place.

Select the straightest piece of decking for the first board and place this board at the ledger side of your deck. Place all decking boards bark or convex side up to minimize cupping and checking (see Figure 41A). The first board should be placed 3/8" from the house wall to allow for drainage.

Be sure to use only hot-dipped galvanized nails (HDG) to fasten decking.

If your budget allows, you can also consider ring shanked nails or spiral nails which are specifi-

cally designed for extra holding power. You might not want any deck nails to show – in that case investigate deck board ties that cannot be seen (see Figure 41H). Finally, you can also use 3" or longer deck screws.

Typically you will use 12 penny HDG common nails for your decking. If you predrill each nailing point, you will avoid splitting the board ends. Drive the nails at an angle (see Figure 41B). For deck screws and ring or spiral nails fasten straight down. Use three nails at board ends or joints and two at the middle joists.

Place remaining decking and be sure to measure and maintain proper 3/16" gap as you go. Set a 16 penny nail between the boards to ensure correct spacing. If your decking doesn't span the complete length of your deck, be sure to alternate the locations of decking joints. Straighten any warped boards with a chisel (see Figures 41C and 41D). When you are 6 feet from placing the last board, begin to vary spacing slightly so that you can avoid ripping a board lengthwise to fit.

When all the decking is in place, snap a chalk line along the outside face of the rim joists. Saw the deck boards at the chalk line so that they are flush with joists (see Figures 41E and 41F).

Figure 40 - Installing Decking Boards

Figure 41A

Lay Boards
Bark Side
Up

Figure 41B

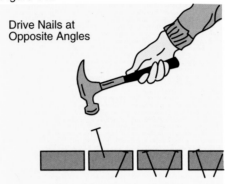

Drive Nails at
Opposite Angles

Figure 41C

Use a Wood Chisel to
Straighten Warped Boards

Figure 41D

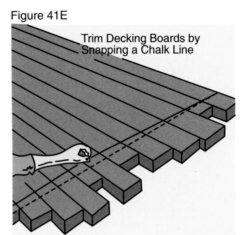

Use a Wood Chisel to
Straighten Warped Boards

Figure 41E

Trim Decking Boards by
Snapping a Chalk Line

Figure 41F

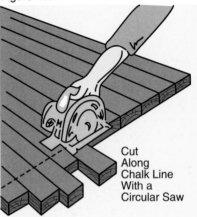

Cut
Along
Chalk Line
With a
Circular Saw

Figure 41G

Measure As You Go

One difficulty you may experience while nailing down deck boards is keeping them parallel. You can solve this problem simply by measuring the distance remaining on the joists from time to time. Take measurements along both sides and the middle as shown below. Tack a string line a foot or two away to serve as a visual guide.

If you discover that some boards are uneven as you continue your work, make your correction gradually by adjusting the space between the next three or four boards.

When you have about six feet of decking left to place, begin adjusting board spacing to avoid an unsightly gap at the end of the deck.

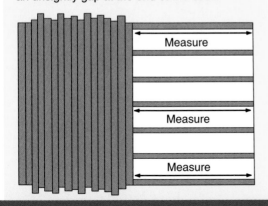

Measure

Measure

Measure

Figure 41H

Deck Board Ties For Installing Deck Boards with NO Surface Nailing

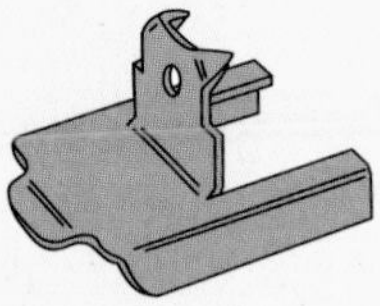

1. Deck Board Tie

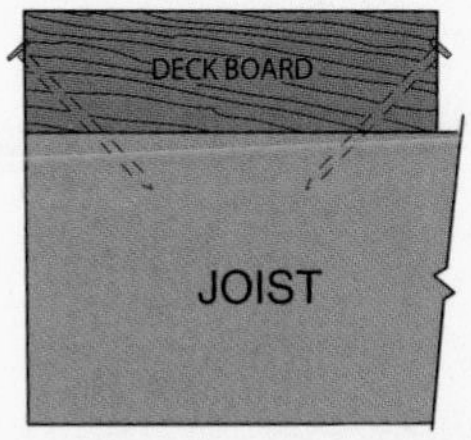

DECK BOARD

JOIST

2. First Deck Board Fastened
to Joist with Toenailing

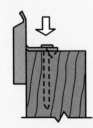

3. Locator Prongs Positions
Deck Tie for Nailing on
Deck Board Edge

4. Slides Under Anchored
Board

FITTING DECKING AROUND POSTS

If you are extending your posts to use as railing members, you will have to notch decking boards to fit around the extended posts. You must remember to support specially cut deck boards at their ends with blocking or cleat support since typically joists will not occur at all the correct positions for nailing.

Consult the illustrations below for methods of supporting decking around notched posts. Measure each side of the post allowing 3/16" on each side as a drainage gap. Use your carpenter's square to mark these measurements on the decking.

You can use either a power saw or a hand saw to make the two perpendicular cuts on your deck board. Next use a broad wood chisel to complete the notch. If you are especially handy with a power reciprocating saw, you can measure an oversize notch with arcs at the corners and use the saw to cut the entire notch in one operation.

Be sure to nail decking properly to supporting joists or cleats around the post. Use 3 nails or 2 deck screws when you fasten decking to supports around the post. Predrill nail holes so that you don't split decking boards.

Figure 42A

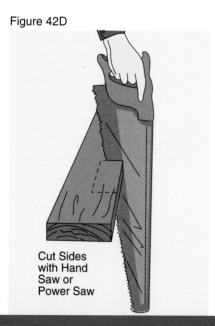

Figure 42B

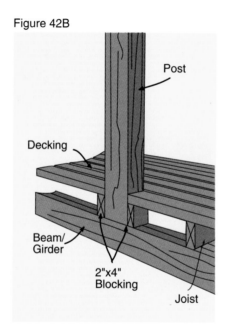

Figure 42C

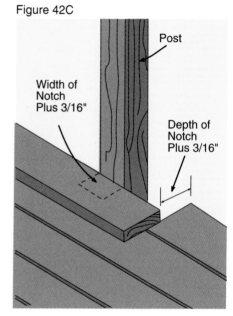

Figure 42D

Figure 42E

Figure 42F

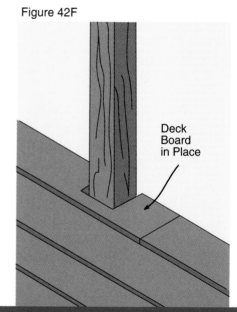

Railings require careful planning before construction begins and should not be added as an afterthought. Consult your local building department for code requirements on railing height, lateral strength, and baluster and rail spacing before you begin construction. Typical railing height is 36" from decking to the top of the cap rail.

First consider if you want to extend deck posts through the decking as major railing supports or if you want to connect 4x4 posts to the rim joists on the perimeter of the deck. See the illustrations at the right for details on these two methods of railing construction.

If you decide to use attached post construction rather than extended post construction, you must attach each post to the rim joist with at least two 3/8" x 5" lag screws and washers at the bottom of the post. For a more finished look, you might want to bevel cut the end of the 4x4 below the screw heads. Predrill the lag screw holes in the post with a 3/8" bit and don't put the holes in the beveled section of the post. Then place the post, checking for plumbness and marking the lag holes with a pencil. Drill these holes with a 1/4" bit and secure the post firmly to the rim joist with lag screws and washers.

Once your railing posts have been cut to the proper height, you will install the cap rail and other horizontal rail members. Cap rails are best constructed from either clear 2x4 or 2x6 boards laid flat. Miter cap rails where they meet at right angles over a post as shown in the illustration at right. Use either a nailing cleat or a metal connector to make a secure connection between rail and post at points below the top of the 4x4.

Toenail rails to posts with 10 penny HDG common nails or use 3 deck screws drilled at a slant. Whatever fastener you employ, don't skimp on quality here. There's nothing more disappointing than rusting fasteners bleeding down your railings and onto your deck surface.

Balusters should be constructed from at least 2x2 material without knots that could make the baluster subject to breakage. Typical baluster spacing is 4" on center depending upon local code requirements. Be sure to keep your balusters plumb and fasten at the top and bottom with either HDG 10 penny common nails or 2-1/2" deck screws which don't require predrilling. If you have beveled the bottom of your attached rail posts, you might want to bevel the tops and bottoms of your balusters for a unified look. If the balusters do not provide the main lateral strength for the rails, you can use finishing nails instead of common nails and then sink the nail heads with a nail punch and cover the heads with an exterior wood putty.

Apply an appropriate wood finish to your completed railing, especially where the end grain of the wood is exposed on cap rails.

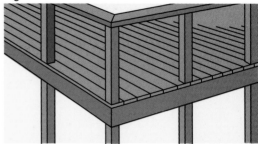

Figure 43A - Extended Post Rail

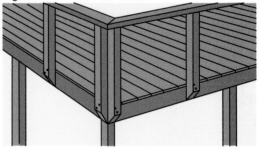

Figure 43B - Rail Post Bolted

Figure 43C - Rail Connection

Mitre at Corner

Metal Anchor

Wood Blocking

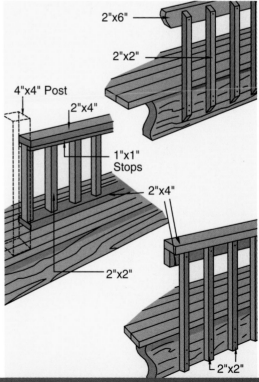

Figure 43D - Popular Railing Styles

2"x6"

2"x2"

4"x4" Post

2"x4"

1"x1" Stops

2"x4"

2"x2"

2"x2"

The illustration below demonstrates one method of attached bench construction that can be added to an existing deck or built when you undertake new deck construction.

There are as many bench options as you can imagine. However, a good guideline for bench construction is that the bench seat should be at least 18" high from the decking and at least 15" deep to provide comfortable seating. A bench with an integrated backrest can be designed to serve a dual purpose on high level decks where it functions as both a seat and a railing.

No matter which bench design you select, you should use clear wood for bench seats which is free from knots, splitting, and other defects.

To construct the bench shown below, fasten two 2x6 bench supports to decking with 12 gauge 8-1/4" long bench support brackets on both sides of the bench supports. Use 1/4" x 1-1/2" lag screws and washers to connect supports to brackets and brackets to decking.

Following the dimensions shown below, cut the seat brace from 2x6 lumber. Secure the seat brace to the seat supports with 3/8" x 5-1/2" carriage bolts with nuts and washers.

Next cut three 2x6s to the correct length and place flatwise on the bench supports. Use 10 penny HDG common nails or 3" deck screws to fasten bench seat boards to bench braces. Leave 1/4" spacing between seat boards for proper drainage. Secure 2x4 trim boards at front and back of bench.

Figure 44 - Bench Construction Diagrams

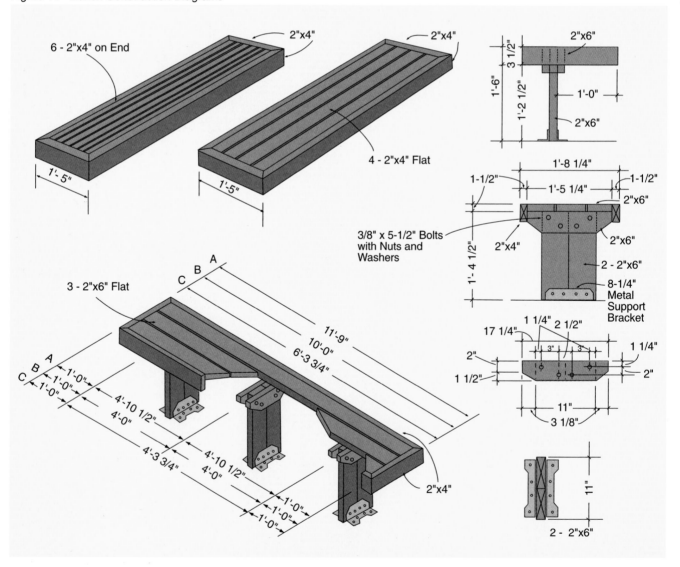

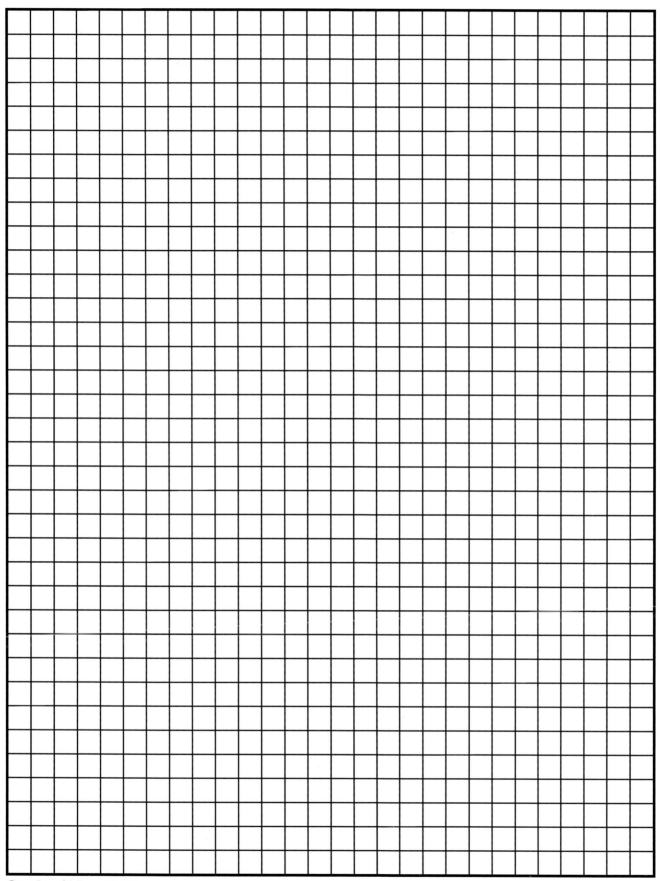

Scale: ¼" = 1'-0" per square

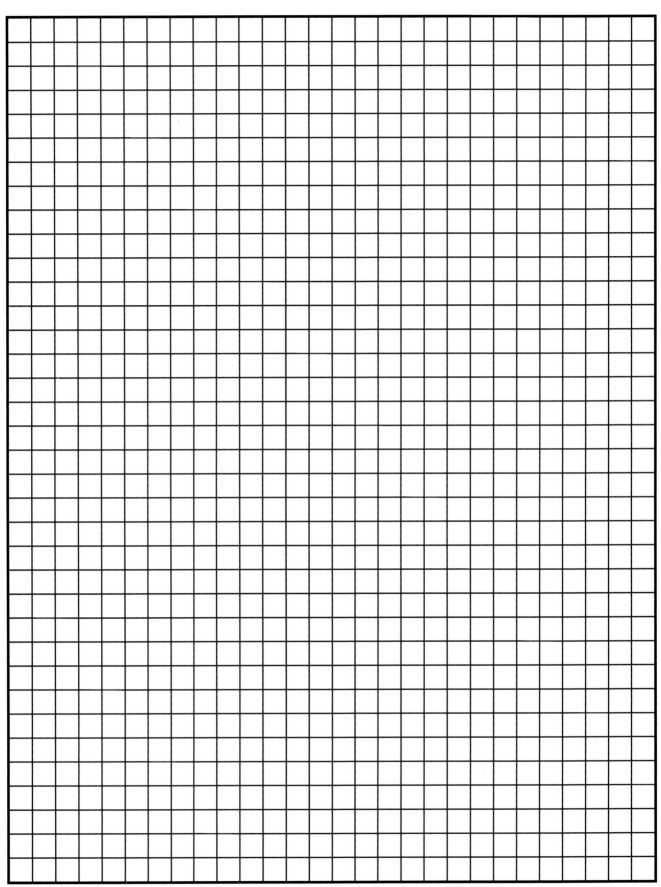

Scale: ¼" = 1'-0" per square

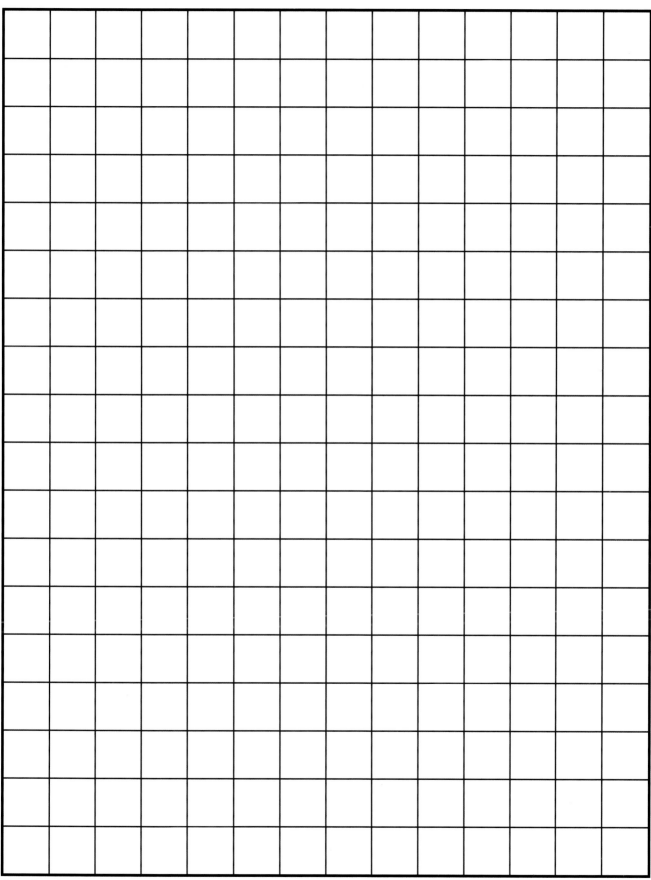

Scale: ½" = 1'-0" per square

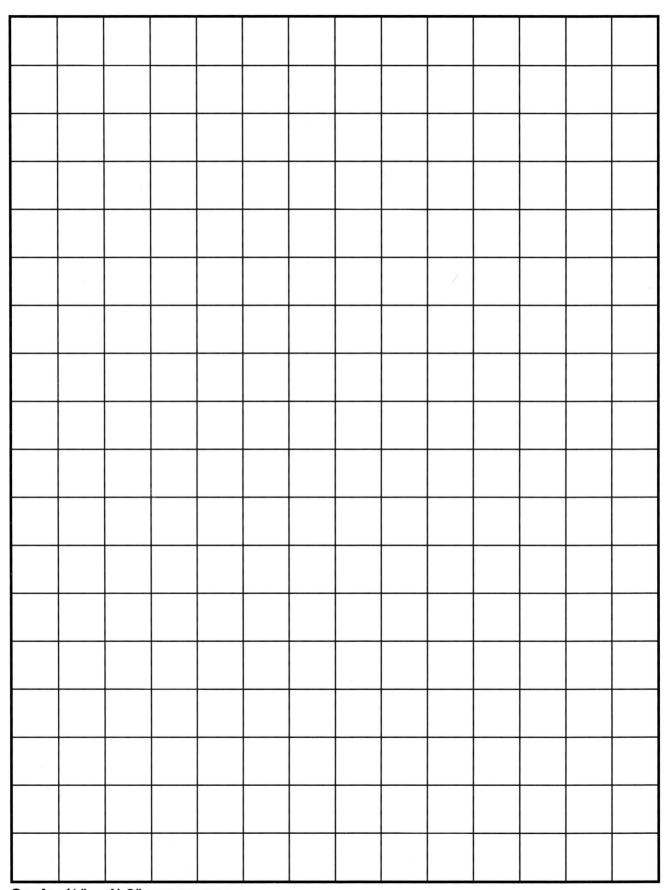

Scale: ½" = 1'-0" per square

GLOSSARY

Anchor - Any metal connector device that is placed in wet concrete and helps to secure posts to piers.

Anchor Bolt - A metal connector device used to connect a wood mudsill to a concrete wall or slab.

Baluster - A vertical railing member typically cut from 2x2 stock that spans top and bottom rails.

Batterboard - Scrap lumber nailed horizontally to stakes driven near each corner of the deck excavation. Stretch nylon strings between batterboards to transfer reference points and to measure elevation.

Beam - Beams are horizontal structural members that are supported by vertical posts. Beams can support joist members on end or decking can be placed directly on beams in certain designs. Typically constructed from 2 or more 2xs or 4x material. See beam span chart for allowable beam spacing and spans. Also called a girder.

Blocking - Material cut from same stock as joist members and nailed between joists for horizontal stability.

Bottom Plate - In stud wall framing, the bottom horizontal member of the wall. Also known as the soleplate.

Bracing - Bracing provides vertical stability to post members on high-level decks. Diagonal bracing should be lag bolted to connecting members for extra stability.

Bridging - Wood or metal cross pieces fastened between joists to provide structural strength and stability.

Cantilever - Refers to the end portion of a joist or the entire portion of the storage building that extends beyond the beam.

Cap Rail - The cap rail is the topmost horizontal railing piece of deck railing. Typically 2x6 or 2x4.

Casing - Molding around door and window openings.

Cleat - A short nailer that supports decking or stair treads.

Codes - Regulations implemented by your local building department that control the design and construction of buildings and other structures such as decks. Consult your local building department for applicable codes before you begin to build your deck or storage building.

Collar Beam - A connecting member used between rafters to strengthen the roof structure.

Cornice - The structure created at the eave overhang which typically consists of fascia board, soffit, and moldings.

Cripple Studs - Short studs that strengthen window and door openings or the gable end of a roof. Also known as jack studs.

Deck Board Tie - A metal fastener that allows you to fasten decking to joists without using nails visible on the surface of the decking.

Deck Screws - A thin-shanked self-drilling screw that is a superior fastener for attaching decking. Especially useful in climates where decking boards must be removed and replaced due to severe weathering.

Decking - Typically 2x4, 2x6, or 5/4" radius edged lumber placed flatwise on 16" or 24" spaced joists. Decking is available in many wood species and grades. Choose your decking material carefully because decking determines the final appearance and durability of your completed deck.

Defect - Any defect in lumber whether as a result of a manufacturing imperfection or an irregularity in the timber from which the lumber was cut. Some defects are blemishes while others can reduce strength and durability. Grading rules establish the extent and severity of wood defects.

Drip Edge - Angled metal or wood located on the outer edge of the roof. Drip edge prevents water penetration.

Drywall - A gypsum panel used to finish interior walls. Also known as plasterboard or sheet rock.

Eave - The roof overhang projecting beyond the exterior wall.

Edge - The narrowest side of a piece of lumber that is perpendicular to both the face and the end.

Elevation - Drawing of your design as it will appear from the front, rear, left and right sides.

Engineered Lumber - Refers to beams or rafters constructed from wood fiber and glue such as glu-lams, micro-lams, or wood I-beams. Often superior in strength and durability to dimensional lumber.

Face - The widest side of a piece of lumber that is perpendicular to both the edge and the end.

Fascia - Trim used along the eave or gable end.

Finish - Any protective coating applied to your deck or storage building to protect against weathering. Finishes are available as stains, paints, or preservatives.

Flakeboard - A panel material made from compressed wood chips bonded with resin. Also known as oriented strand board (OSB) or chipboard.

Flashing - Metal material used on the roof and eaves to prevent moisture penetration.

Fly Rafters - Rafters at the gable end which "fly" unsupported by the tie plate. Also known as rack, barge, or verge rafters.

Footing - Concrete footings help to anchor your piers in the surrounding soil and distribute weight over a larger surface area. In climates where the soil freezes, a generous footing protects against soil heaves and movement of your storage building.

Frieze - A horizontal framing member that connects the siding with the soffit.

Frost Line - Measure of the maximum penetration of frost in the soil in a given geographic location. Depth of frost penetration varies with climate conditions.

Furring - Narrow strips of wood attached to walls or other surfaces that serve as a fastening base for drywall.

Gable - The triangular end of the roof structure formed by the roof framing.

Galvanized Nails - Hot-dipped galvanized nails (HDG) are dipped in zinc and will not rust.

Girder - Same as beam.

Grade Stamp - A stamp imprinted on dimensional lumber that identifies wood species, grade texture, moisture content, and usage. Grade descriptions such as select, finish, and common signify limiting characteristics that may occur in lumber in each grade. The stamp indicates a uniform measurement of performance that permits lumber of a given grade to be used for the same purpose, regardless of the manufacturer.

Grading - The process of excavating, leveling, and compacting the soil or gravel beneath your deck or storage building to its desired finish level. Proper grading avoids drainage problems.

Grain - Lumber shows either a flat or vertical grain depending on how it was cut from the log. To minimize warping along the face of the deck or storage building (known as cupping) and raising of the grain, you should place flat grain with the bark side up or facing out.

Gravel - Granular rock material that varies in size from approximately 1/4" to 3" in diameter. Results from either natural disintegration of stone or crushing and processing of rock.

Header - A horizontal load-bearing support member over an opening in the wall such as window or door openings.

Heartwood - Core of the log that resists decay.

Hip Rafter - A short rafter that forms the hip of a roof and runs from the corner of a wall to the ridge board. Usually set at a 45-degree angle to the walls.

Jack Rafter - A short rafter that runs from the ridge board to a hip or valley rafter or from the hip rafter to the tie plate.

Joist - Typically 2x lumber which is set on edge and supports your deck or storage building. Joists in turn are supported by beams, ledgers, and rim joists. See joist span chart on page 13 for maximum allowable joist spacing and spans for a given joist size.

Joist Hanger - A metal connector available in many sizes and styles that attaches to a ledger or rim joist and makes a secure butt joint between ledger and joist.

Lag Screw - Heavy-duty fastener with hexagonal bolt head that provides extra fastening power for railing posts, ledgers, and other critical structural connections. Use galvanized lag screws and washers to prevent rust.

Ledger - The ledger board is attached with lag screws to the side of your house in attached deck construction. The ledger supports joists that are attached to the ledger with joist hangers.

Let-in Brace - Usually a 1x4 corner brace in a wall section that runs diagonally from the bottom to top plate.

Live Load - The predetermined load that a deck is capable of supporting expressed in pounds per square foot. Live load includes moving and variable loads such as people, furniture, or portable spas.

Lookout - Blocking which extends from an inner common rafter to the fly rafters at the gable ends.

Metal Connectors - Used to augment or replace nails as fasteners, metal connectors are critical for lasting and sturdy deck and storage building construction.

Moisture Content - Moisture content of wood is the weight of water in wood expressed as a percentage of the weight of wood from which all water has been removed. The drier the lumber the less the lumber will shrink and warp on your finished deck or storage building. Surfaced lumber with a moisture content of 19% results in a "S-GRN" stamp to indicate surfaced green. Avoid green lumber especially when selecting your boards.

Mudsill - The part of the wall framing that contacts the foundation. Should be pressure-treated to resist moisture and decay. Also known as the sill plate.

Outrigger - An extension of a rafter at the eave used to form a cornice or overhang on a roof.

Pea Gravel - Approximately 1/4" round gravel material which can be used in a 4"-6" layer to cover the soil under your deck or storage building. Provides drainage and prevents soil-to-wood contact for decks or storage buildings built on sleepers rather than piers.

Perimeter - Outside boundary of the structure.

Perpendicular - At a 90 degree or right angle.

Pier - Piers support the total weight load of your deck or storage building and anchor the structure to the soil. Concrete piers can either be precast in a pyramidal shape with a nailing block on top or poured in place. Precast piers are typically used in climates where the soil does not freeze hard. Poured in place piers are utilized where the soil freezes and must extend a certain depth below the frost line. Either precast or poured in place piers should have adequate footings to prevent movement of the pier in the soil. Consult your local building department for requirements regarding pier type and placement.

Pilot Hole - A slightly undersized hole drilled in lumber that prevents splitting of the wood when nailed.

Pitch - A measurement of roof slope. Expressed as the ratio of the total rise divided by the span.

Plumb - Absolutely vertical. Determined with either a plumb bob or spirit level.

Post - The vertical support that bears the weight of the joists and beams. Typically posts are at least 4x4 lumber. When post height exceeds a limit defined by your local building code, posts must be stabilized by bracing. Vertical railing supports are also known as posts.

Pressure-Treated - Refers to the process of forcing preservative compounds into the fiber of the wood. Handle pressure-treated lumber with caution and do not inhale or burn its sawdust. Certain types of pressure-treated lumber are suitable for ground contact use while others must be used above ground. While more expensive than untreated lumber, pressure-treated wood resists decay and is recommended where naturally decay-resistant species like cedar or redwood are unavailable or too costly.

Purlin - A horizontal member of the roof framing that supports rafters or spans between trusses.

Rafter - A roof framing member that extends from the top plate to the ridge board and supports the roof sheeting and roofing material.

Rail - Any horizontal railing member.

Rake - The inclined end area of a gable roof.

Redwood - Decay-resistant and stable wood for long-lasting storage building construction. Redwood grades from best to worst are: Clear All Heart (no knots), Construction Heart (small knots), Construction Common (sapwood), Merchantable Heart (knots and knotholes), and Merchantable (sapwood with knots and knotholes). Heart grades provide the greatest decay resistance.

Reinforcing Bar - A steel rod that provides internal reinforcement for concrete piers. Also known as rebar.

Ridge Board - A 1x or typically 2x member on edge at the roof's peak to which the rafters are connected.

Right Triangle, 3-4-5 - A means of ensuring squareness when you lay out your structure. Mark a vertical line at exactly 4'-0" from the angle you want to square. Then mark a horizontal line at exactly 3'-0" from the crossing vertical line. Measure the distance diagonally between both the 3' and 4' marks and when the distance measures exactly 5'-0" you have squared a 90 degree angle between lines. Also works as a 6-8-10 right triangle.

Rim Joist - A perimeter joist to which the deck and storage building joists are attached.

Rise - Refers to the vertical height between each step in stair construction. In roof construction, the vertical distance the ridge rises above the top plate at the center of the span.

Rough Sill - The lowest framing member of a door or window opening.

Sapwood - Outer layers of growth between the bark and heartwood. Less decay-resistant than heartwood.

Scale - A system of representation in plan drawing where small dimensions represent an equivalent large dimension. In typical deck and storage building plans the drawings are said to be scaled down. Scale is expressed as an equation such as 1/4" = 1'-0"

Screed - A straight piece of lumber used to level wet concrete or the gravel.

Sheathing - Exterior sheet (typically 4'x8') material fastened to the rafter or exterior stud walls.

Skid - Typically a decay-resistant 4x4 member which is placed horizontally on the ground or gravel bed and which supports the storage building flooring. Recommended use is only in dry climates with stable soil.

Sleeper - Typically a decay-resistant 4x4 member which is placed horizontally on the ground or gravel bed and which supports decking. Recommended use is only in dry climates with stable soil.

Slope - A measurement of ground inclination and expressed as a percentage of units of vertical rise per 100 units of horizontal distance.

Soffit - The underside of the roof overhang. Soffits can either be closed or open (thus exposing the roof rafters).

Spacing - The distance between joist members and measured from center to center.

Span - The distance between beam supports which is measured center to center.

Spirit Level - A sealed cylinder with a transparent tube nearly filled with liquid forming a bubble used to indicate true vertical and horizontal alignment when the bubble is centered in the length of the tube.

Stair Stringer - An inclined 2x member that supports the treads of a stair. Stringers can be notched with a template pattern or unnotched where treads are supported with metal step support brackets. Also known as carriage or riser.

Step Support - Step supports are 10-1/4" or 8-1/4" long specially configured brackets made from 12 gauge galvanized structural grade steel. They make it easier to build stairs when it is necessary to adjust the angle of the stringers to span the distance between the deck and the ground.

String Level - A spirit level mounted in a frame with prongs at either end for hanging on a string. Determines level across string lines.

Stud - The vertical framing member of a wall.

T1-11 siding - Exterior siding material with vertical grooves usually 8" on center.

Texture - Refers to the surface finish of lumber.

Tie Plate - The framing member nailed to the top plates in order to connect and align wall sections. Also known as the cap plate or second top plate.

Toenail - To drive a nail at an angle. When you toenail a post to a beam for example, you should drive the nail so that one-half the nail is in each member.

Tongue and Groove - Refers to the milling of lumber so that adjacent parts interlock for added strength and durability.

Top Plate - The horizontal top part of the wall framing perpendicular to the wall studs.

Tread - Treads provide the horizontal stepping surface in stair construction. To ensure against tread breakage, use clear 2x wood without knots for treads.

Trim Board - A nonstructural board that covers the end of decking boards or is abutted to the rim joist. To prevent warping, you can attach trim boards with screws.

Trimmer Stud - The stud adjacent to window or door opening studs which strengthens the opening and bears the weight of the window or door headers. Also known as a jack stud.

Truss - A triangular prefabricated unit for supporting a roof load over a span. Trusses are relatively lightweight and can offer an easier method of roof construction for the novice.

Valley Rafter - A rafter running from a tie plate at the corner of a wall along the roof valley and up to the ridge.

Zinc-Coated - Refers to fasteners coated with zinc, a non-corrosive metal used as a galvanizing material.

Building your own storage building can be a simple project if the proper planning and guidelines are followed. More and more, people are turning to do-it-yourself projects as a means of completing additions and renovations to their houses, so why not build your own storage building?

A storage building can significantly increase the value of your property while maintaining a well organized yard. Plus, the additional storage will make all your household chores easier and less time consuming. Maybe your family needs a children's playhouse, or perhaps you need more of a utility building for yard or farm equipment. Whatever your needs, this section of storage project plans has it all.

BUILD YOUR OWN STORAGE BUILDING?

The answer is YES! By doing the planning and all or part of the work yourself, you can have the storage building you might not otherwise be able to afford. By supplying the labor and buying materials yourself, construction costs can be cut significantly.

Framing out a storage building is not difficult. Standardized materials and construction techniques make it relatively easy if you take time to plan and work carefully.

The key to a successful storage building project is planning, planning, and more planning! Once you have begun construction of your storage building, it is both costly and time-consuming to correct errors in storage building placement, construction, or selection of materials. So the motto of the Do-It-Yourself storage building builder must be **PLAN AHEAD!** Whether you choose to draw the plans for your storage building following the guidelines in this manual or you decide to purchase a pre-drawn storage building plan that is offered on pages 116-127, you must carefully plan all elements of your storage building project.

Here is a checklist of design information which you must gather before you begin to design your storage building:

❏ **Local Building Requirements -** Visit your local building department and determine how local building codes and zoning ordinances will influence your project. Be prepared to apply for a building permit once you have completed your design.

❏ **Deed Restrictions -** Are there conditions in your property deed that restrict the type and location of your storage building? Are you planning to place your storage building over property controlled by an easement for right-of-way or utility access?

❏ **Climatic Factors -** Evaluate the microclimate of your intended storage building location. Microclimate includes the shading effect of deciduous or evergreen trees and shrubs, the angle of the sun in relation to nearby landscaping during different seasons, soil drainage conditions, and prevailing wind and temperature conditions. Remember that an enclosed storage building without temperature regulation needs to be protected from the sun in the summer and exposed to any available in the winter.

❏ **Storage Building Functions -** What do you want your storage building to do? Will your storage building serve as a simple storage building for gardening and lawn tools or do you plan to use the storage building to store household items? Do you want to supply the shed with electrical power? What type of storage or shelving units would you like to install in your completed storage building? Will your storage building include a workshop or hobby area? Careful planning regarding the functions of your shed will save you from costly changes after the project is completed.

❏ **Plan Carefully BEFORE You Begin -** All the techniques and tips you'll need are in this book. Read it carefully before you begin construction. It will help you determine the work you can handle alone and also where expert help might be needed to do the job right. You can also learn many construction basics by studying existing storage buildings. Ask your neighbors if you can take a few minutes to review their storage buildings before you begin planning your design.

❏ **Your Budget -** You must determine an estimated dollar amount that you plan to spend on your storage building. Do you plan to construct the storage building yourself or will you subcontract with a professional to build the storage building after you have purchased materials? Perhaps you want a contractor to complete your storage building project in its entirety. It is helpful if you can set upper and lower spending limits so that you can consider options in the materials that you plan for your storage building. If you decide to finance your storage building project, don't forget to include interest cost in the total cost amount.

❏ **Your Materials Source -** After you have completed your design work and have settled on a bill of materials, you should remember that a helpful Menards store is an invaluable resource for the successful completion of your storage building project. Consult with the Menards Building Material Desk for all the materials you require. If special ordering is necessary, determine lead times. Don't underestimate the importance of a reputable Menards store in providing both quality materials and design knowledge.

The storage building site plans on this page are included to exemplify how your storage building can contribute valuable storage space to your home. Before you place your storage building on your property, study traffic patterns in your backyard and how often you will use the building on a daily basis. Create a site plan of your property and draw arrows to illustrate the basic movements to and from your home. Establish priorities for storage locations and traffic to your proposed storage building.

Be aware of problem areas that relate to storage building placement. Will you need to build a ramp to move lawn tools in and out of the building? Be certain that you have adequate clearances to move these tools up and down the ramp. If your storage building uses clerestory windows for example to supplement or replace electrical lighting, remember that south-facing windows will provide the greatest amount of natural lighting.

Study the site plans shown in Figures 54A to 54D for ideas concerning storage building placement. If you create a site plan of your own, remember that it is essential to locate exterior doors and windows on your plan. Try to include all exterior structures and landscaping in your plan. While a scale drawing is not essential, it is not difficult to create a site plan to scale with a ruler and pencil. Grid paper with 1/4" grids is perfect for drawing your preliminary site plan on a 1/4"=1'-0" scale.

These site plans are provided for illustration purposes only. You should sketch your own site plan first and make certain that your proposed storage building addition conforms to all applicable building codes before you begin construction. A little time devoted to planning before you begin will save time and money during the construction of your project.

Figure 54B

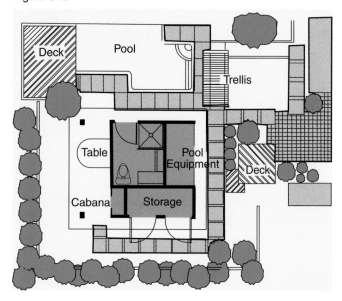

Figure 54C

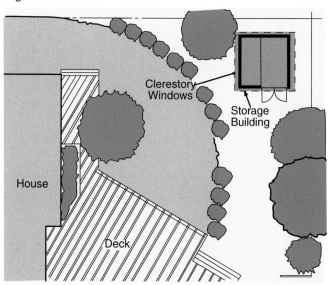

Figure 54A

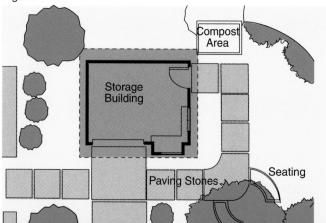

Figure 54D

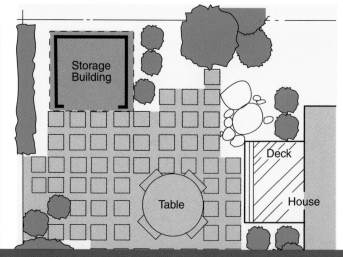

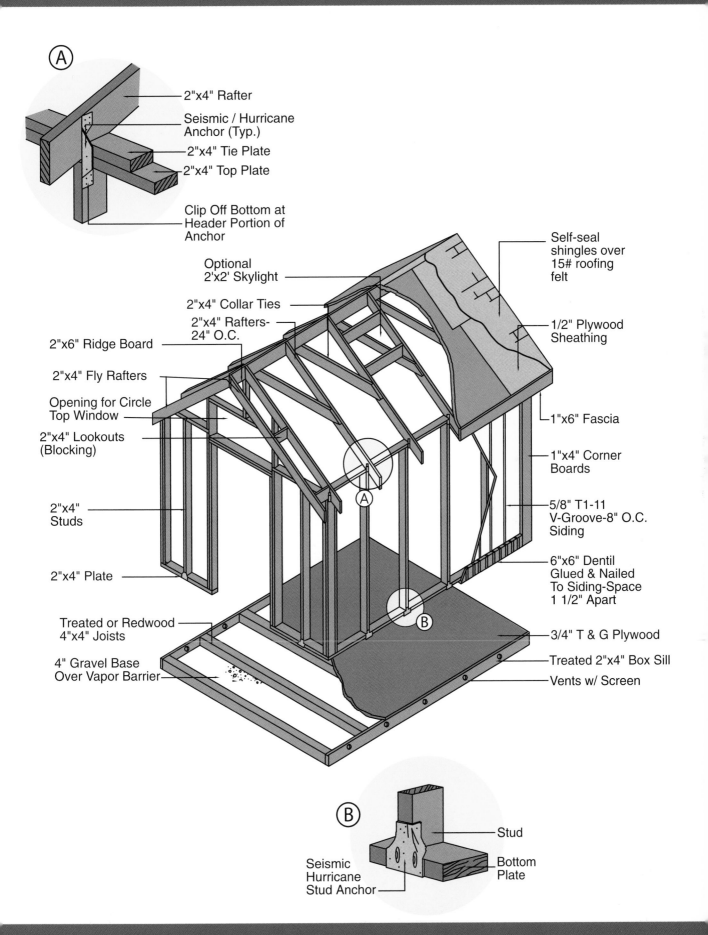

A
- 2"x4" Rafter
- Seismic / Hurricane Anchor (Typ.)
- 2"x4" Tie Plate
- 2"x4" Top Plate
- Clip Off Bottom at Header Portion of Anchor

- Optional 2'x2' Skylight
- 2"x4" Collar Ties
- 2"x4" Rafters- 24" O.C.
- 2"x6" Ridge Board
- 2"x4" Fly Rafters
- Opening for Circle Top Window
- 2"x4" Lookouts (Blocking)
- 2"x4" Studs
- 2"x4" Plate
- Treated or Redwood 4"x4" Joists
- 4" Gravel Base Over Vapor Barrier

- Self-seal shingles over 15# roofing felt
- 1/2" Plywood Sheathing
- 1"x6" Fascia
- 1"x4" Corner Boards
- 5/8" T1-11 V-Groove-8" O.C. Siding
- 6"x6" Dentil Glued & Nailed To Siding-Space 1 1/2" Apart
- 3/4" T & G Plywood
- Treated 2"x4" Box Sill
- Vents w/ Screen

B
- Stud
- Bottom Plate
- Seismic Hurricane Stud Anchor

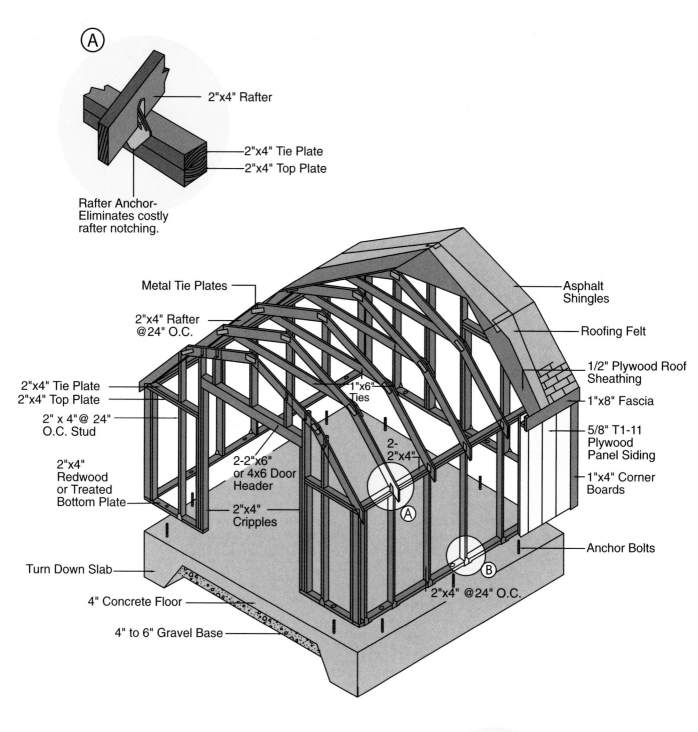

Ⓐ

2"x4" Rafter

2"x4" Tie Plate
2"x4" Top Plate

Rafter Anchor-
Eliminates costly
rafter notching.

Metal Tie Plates

2"x4" Rafter
@24" O.C.

2"x4" Tie Plate
2"x4" Top Plate

2" x 4" @ 24"
O.C. Stud

2"x4"
Redwood
or Treated
Bottom Plate

2-2"x6"
or 4x6 Door
Header

2"x4"
Cripples

1"x6"
Ties

2-
2"x4"

Ⓐ

Ⓑ

2"x4" @24" O.C.

Asphalt
Shingles

Roofing Felt

1/2" Plywood Roof
Sheathing

1"x8" Fascia

5/8" T1-11
Plywood
Panel Siding

1"x4" Corner
Boards

Anchor Bolts

Turn Down Slab

4" Concrete Floor

4" to 6" Gravel Base

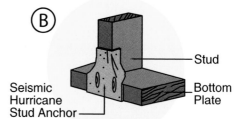

Ⓑ

Stud

Bottom
Plate

Seismic
Hurricane
Stud Anchor

CHOOSING THE RIGHT LOCATION

Before you begin, consult with your local building department and obtain information regarding the placement, height, and square footage of outdoor storage buildings. For example, your local codes might specify that outbuildings cannot exceed a certain peak to ground height and that a storage building must be offset a certain distance from property lines. If you disregard the code restrictions in your municipality, you will create problems for yourself and your neighbors. You might even be forced to remove a structure that violates local code requirements or to pay fines. If your local code requires a permit, submit a site plan and storage building construction plans to your local building department and obtain all necessary permits before you begin construction.

Remember that your storage building will serve as an important storage addition to your home. With this goal in mind, be certain to select a location that will make storage building access convenient but unobtrusive. Sketch a traffic plan that details major access paths in your yard and around your home to help you determine the correct location for your storage building.

Consider the building location in relationship to existing and future elements of your landscaping. Don't build a storage building next to a tree whose growing roots will displace the storage building foundation. Be certain that the placement of your storage building in your backyard landscape matches the planned use of the storage building. For example, if you want to use the storage building in the winter, don't place the storage building on the north side of a large evergreen tree which would completely block valuable winter sunlight.

If at all possible, always select a well-drained location for your storage building. A spot with poor drainage or soft ground will cause problems later. Water accumulating under the storage building creates condensation and can rust the materials you are storing inside.

LAYOUT OF STORAGE BUILDING SITE

Accurately locating the four corners of the building will in turn establish the boundaries for the foundation. The site is laid out using batterboards set back from the corners of the planned building in an L-shaped arrangement. Setting the batterboards back from the actual building site allows you to maintain an accurate reference point as you dig footings and construct the foundation (see Figure 57).

Batterboards are made of pointed stakes connected with 4' lengths of 1x4 lumber. Each batterboard should form an accurate right angle when checked with a framing square. Batterboard tops must be level with each other all the way around. Check for levelness with a string level or a mason's line level. Consult the step-by-step instructions on page 58 for help in establishing your site layout.

A variety of storage building foundation construction methods are available depending upon your local site and your budget. If you do not want to anchor the storage building permanently to one location, consider the wood skids and wood floor foundation detailed on page 59. Alternative foundation options are detailed on pages 60 and 61.

For example, in areas where the ground does not freeze during the winter, pier block foundations offer an inexpensive and sturdy method of anchoring your storage building foundation. Pre-cast pier blocks with nailers are readily available at many building supply retailers and provide a relatively simple foundation base for the first time builder.

A more expensive and permanent alternative foundation is the turned-down or monolithic concrete slab. Concrete has the advantage of durability and resistance to moisture damage. If you do select a concrete slab, make sure that your slab will drain properly if moisture is released within your storage building. Drainage for concrete slabs is especially important for cabana or greenhouse structures.

Figure 57 - Batterboards

Figure 58 - Layout Procedure

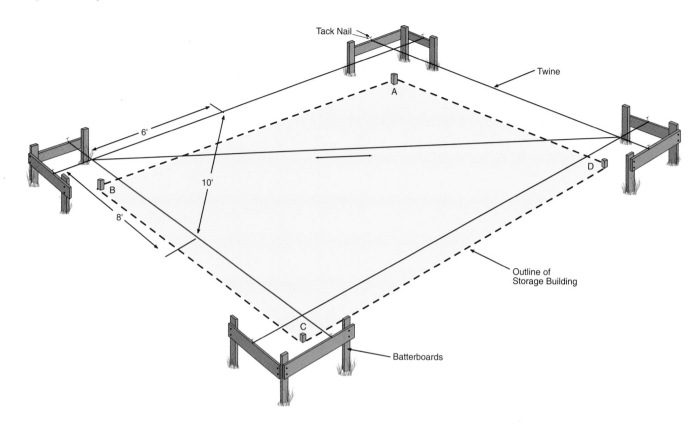

1. Accurately locate one corner of the building and drive stake A at that point (see Figure 58).
2. Measure out along the long side of the building to the next corner. Drive in stake B at this point. Drive a small nail into the stakes and connect with tightly drawn twine.
3. Measure out the approximate positions of corners C and D and drive stakes at these points. Use a framing square to form an approximate right angle at these corners. Run twine from stakes B to C, C to D, and D to A.
4. You will now erect batterboards and adjust stake locations to form a true square or rectangular layout. Erect batterboards so that each corner stake is lined up directly on the diagonal from the opposite corner as illustrated. Use the line level to check that all batterboards are level with each other.
5. Stretch mason's twine between the batterboards so it is aligned directly over stakes A and B. When perfectly aligned make a saw kerf in the batterboards to make a permanent reference point and tack down the twine taut.
6. Stretch twine over stakes B and C. It must form a perfect right angle with twine A-B. Check for a perfect right angle using the 6-8-10 method. Measure 6'-0" out along twine A-B and 8'-0" along twine B-C. Mark these points with pins. The diagonal between these two pins should measure exactly 10'-0". Adjust the position of twine B-C until the diagonal does equal 10'-0" and then notch the batterboard at stake C and fasten off line B-C.
7. Using the 6-8-10 method lay out twine C-D and D-A. At each corner carefully measure from the point where the twine lines cross each other to set building dimensions. Drop a plumb line at this intersecting point and set stakes in exact positions.
8. Check the final layout by measuring the diagonals between foundation stakes. The diagonals must be equal in length if your layout is squared up. If they are not, recheck your measurement and make proper adjustments.

Figure 59 - Skid and Wood Floor Foundation

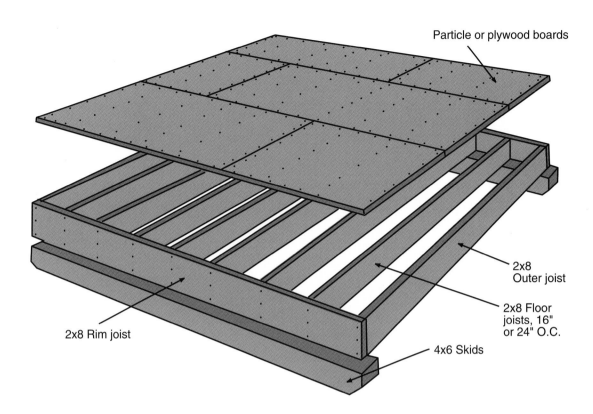

Particle or plywood boards

2x8 Outer joist

2x8 Floor joists, 16" or 24" O.C.

2x8 Rim joist

4x6 Skids

1. **Site Preparation** - Prepare the site by scraping away all grass or weed material covering the storage building area. If your soil does not drain well, remove 4"- 6" of earth under the storage building area and replace with 4" of pea gravel to increase drainage. Otherwise you can simply dig a drainage trench approximately 12" wide by 6" deep where the 4x6 skids are to be placed. Fill the drainage trench with gravel to ensure good drainage and to minimize the wood to soil contact.

2. **Placing the Skids** - Skids should be either pressure treated or redwood to prevent decay from ground contact. Position the 4x6 skids and make certain that the skids are level (see Figure 59). Tie the skids together by nailing the outer 2x8 floor joist to the front and rear rim joist. Toenail the outer joist to the skid. If you want to incline the storage building floor slightly to ensure drainage, you should raise one end of both skids by an equal amount (1" for every 8' of skid) by placing additional gravel under the skid.

3. **Constructing the Floor Frame** - Having nailed the rim joist to the skids, you should now check that the floor frame is square. You can use the 6-8-10 method detailed on page 58 to ensure squareness. Complete the floor framing by adding the remaining 2x8 floor joists placed at 16" on center. Connect the floor joists to the rim joists with at least 3-16d coated sinkers at each end. If your budget allows it, use metal joist hangers to add extra strength to your floor joist framing.

4. **Adding the Flooring** - For extra strength and durability, use 4'x8'x3/4" tongue and groove exterior grade plywood for flooring. For normal use, install 4'x8'x3/4" CDX plywood to construct your floor. Fasten the floor framing to the floor joists using 8d nails 6" on center at the edge of the sheets and 10" on center along the intermediate floor joists. Take care to construct a stable and even floor which will serve as the foundation for your wall sections.

1. **Site Preparation** - Prepare the site by scraping away all grass or weed material covering the storage building area. If your soil does not drain well, remove 4"-6" of earth and replace with 4" of pea gravel to increase drainage.

2. **Locating the Piers** - You will need to use your batterboards (see pages 57-58) to stretch a nylon string along the imaginary outer wall line. Use this string line to stake the pier locations at 4'-0" on center (see Figure 60). The piers will support either a 4x6 beam or a built-up beam made from two 2x6s.

3. **Pre-cast Piers** - If you are using precast concrete piers with an attached wooden nailer, you need to dig a pier footing at least 14" wide and 6" deep. The depth of the footing should be at least 6" below the local frost line. Pour the concrete into the footing hole. Spray the pier with water and then embed the pier at least 3" into the fresh concrete and twist slightly to achieve a solid bond between the concrete and the pier. Make certain that you have enough concrete in the hole so that the top of the nailer block is at least 4"-6" above grade level. Check the alignment of the pier by dropping a plumb bob from the centerline string. Finally, use a level across the block and tap the pier until it is level in all directions and square.

4. **Attach the Beam Support Posts to the Piers** - Cut 4x4 beam support posts to place the floor at a height above grade determined by local codes. If you don't require posts, simply toenail the 4x6 beam into the precast pier nailer blocks with 12d coated sinkers. If you require a certain grade to floor clearance, toenail the posts into the nailer and then use a post cap connector to secure the beam to the post.

5. **Constructing the Floor Framing and Floor** - Follow the methods outlined in steps 3 and 4 on page 59 to construct the floor framing and the wood floor.

Figure 60 - Concrete Pier and Wood Floor Foundation

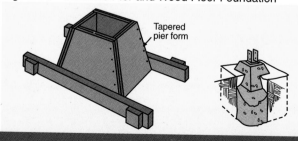

Optional Poured In-Place Piers - First be certain you have purchased enough concrete to complete pier installation. Concrete is measured in cubic yards. To calculate the concrete required for a given number of cylindrical piers, use the following formula to find the Total Volume in cubic yards:

$$\text{Volume} = \frac{3.14 \times \text{Depth of Pier (feet)} \times \text{Diameter (feet)} \times \text{Diameter (feet)} \times \text{No. Piers}}{108}$$

Example: Concrete required for twelve 10" diameter piers, 30" deep.

$$\text{Volume in cubic yards} = \frac{3.14 \times 2.5 \times .83 \times .83 \times 12}{108} = 0.61$$

*Remember to convert inches to feet (10 inches = .83 feet)
Conversion Factor: 27 Cubic Feet = 1 Cubic Yard

Mix concrete according to manufacturer's instructions in a wheelbarrow or in a "half-bag" mixer. Use clean water for mixing and achieve the proper plastic consistency before you pour the concrete. If you are not using ready-mix concrete, prepare a 1:2:3 mix – one part concrete, two parts river sand, and three parts gravel.

Coat the inside of the forms with oil to prevent sticking and dampen the inside of the hole with water before you pour the concrete.

With your post base anchors at hand, pour the concrete into the forms and tap slightly to settle. For poured in-place piers, wait for the concrete to begin to harden and set the post base anchors into the concrete. Ensure that anchors are square and level. You can drop a plumb bob from your centerline string to be certain that your anchor is centered properly. Adjust post base anchors to the correct height.

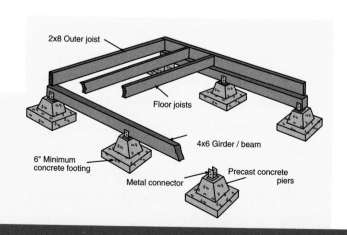

CONCRETE SLAB FOUNDATION

Figure 61 - Concrete Slab Foundation

Figure 61 - Concrete Slab Foundation

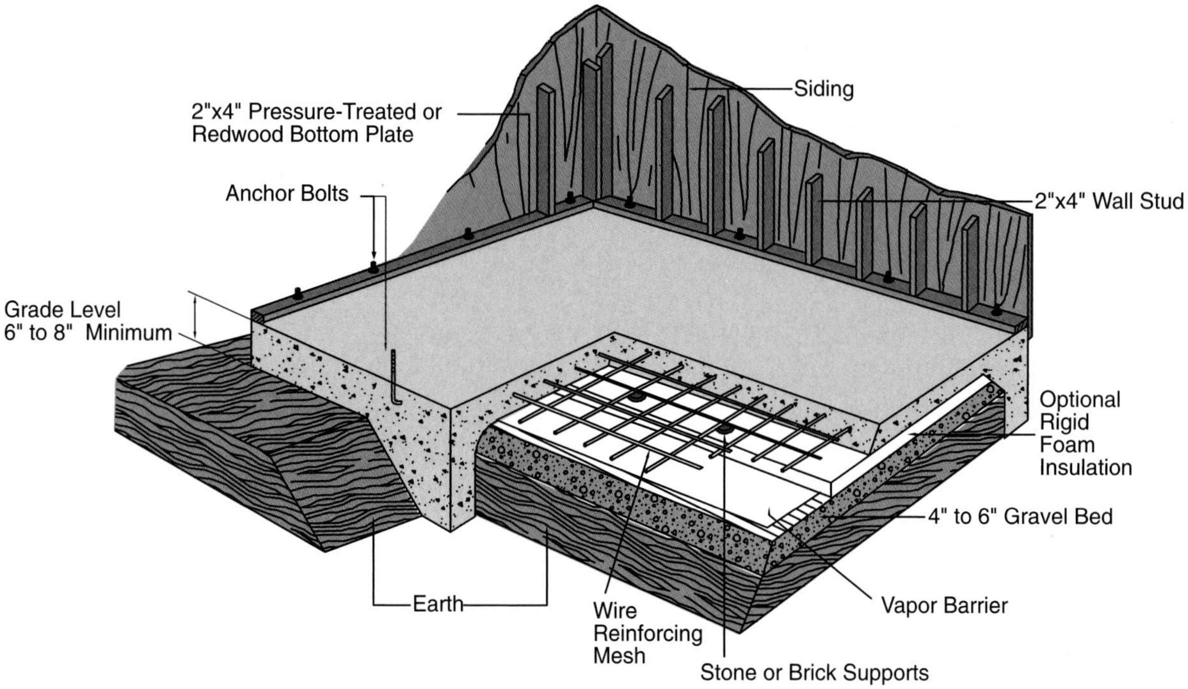

A concrete slab is the most permanent and durable method of constructing a foundation for your storage building. However, slab construction requires greater preparation and expense than wood floor construction using skids or concrete piers.

1. **Site Preparation** - Prepare the site by scraping away all grass or weed material covering the storage building area. Stake out the area for the slab. Be certain that all corners are square. If you are using a plan for slab construction, remember that all dimensions on the plan are to the outside of concrete. Excavate 4" of soil over storage building area and replace with 4" of gravel to ensure proper drainage under slab. Level the gravel fill (see Figure 61).

2. **Digging the Footing** - Dig a trench for the slab footing approximately 8" wide at bottom and tapering inward to approximately 16" wide at top. The footing should extend down about 12" or at least 6" below the local frost line.

3. **Building the Forms** - Use 2" scrap lumber to build the forms for the slab. Set the top of the 2" form board to the desired floor height and level. The inside face of form boards must line up exactly with "string lines" set at proper building dimensions. Brace your forms securely since you don't want them to shift or break when concrete is poured.

4. **Preparing to Pour the Concrete** - Place a 6 mil plastic vapor barrier over the gravel bed before you pour. Overlap the plastic sheets by at least 12" and do not puncture the plastic. If you want to insulate your slab from the earth, place 1" rigid foam insulation over the plastic provided that you have allowed for the additional height. Add two levels of 1/2" reinforcing bar (rebar) to the top and bottom of the footing and secure the rebar with tie wire held by nails in the forms. Finally place 6"x6" reinforcing wire mesh over the slab area and support the mesh with small wooden or masonry blocks so that it rests 2" above the vapor barrier.

5. **Estimating the Concrete** - The table to the right will help you estimate the approximate amount of concrete required to create a 4" thick slab with 18" deep footings.

Estimating Concrete

Slab Size	Concrete Required
8' x 12'	2.5 cubic yards
12' x 12'	3.5 cubic yards
12' x 16'	5.0 cubic yards
12' x 20'	6.0 cubic yards

If necessary, have your local building inspector approve the forms before you pour. If your storage building will utilize electrical service or plumbing, place the electrical conduit or plumbing in the proper location before you pour.

Placing

Be prepared for the arrival of the ready-mix truck or you could be charged a wait time fee. Have extra helpers, wheelbarrow, and concrete finishing tools ready. When the truck arrives, pour the area farthest from the truck and fill the footing trench making sure the concrete does not push the forms or rebar out of alignment. For larger areas, break the work into smaller sections by installing temporary screeding guides.

When one section is poured move to the next section while the helpers screed off the first. Ask a helper to knock the sides of the forms with a hammer in order to force air pockets out of the concrete. Be sure that all voids are filled with concrete. Pay special attention to the perimeter area of the form boards. Remove the temporary screed guides when you fill in these voids.

Finishing

Once the concrete has lost its initial shine, begin finishing it with a bull float. Larger floats have a handle like a broom. If you are using smaller hand floats, use toe and knee boards placed on the concrete so you can kneel on the concrete without leaving much of an impression. Move the float in long sweeping motions.

Anchor bolts should be placed after the concrete has been screeded and bull floated. Place the bolts 1-3/4" away from the edge of the slab. Double-check spacing of bolts and alignment.

For a coarser finish, bull floating is all that is required. For a slicker, smoother finish, use a steel trowel to go over the work once bull floating is complete. Use a light touch so you don't gouge the concrete surface. Before the concrete hardens completely, take a trowel and cut between the edge of the concrete and the form.

Curing

Once all finishing is completed, mist down the slab with water, and cover it with a layer of plastic or burlap. Keep the surface moist for four days as the concrete cures.

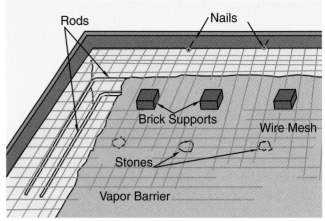

Figure 62A - Steel reinforcing rods and wire mesh are laid into place over gravel and optional plastic vapor barrier.

Figure 62B - Workers level concrete slab with a screed board.

Figure 62C - Smooth concrete surface with a bull float.

Figure 62D - Add anchor bolts.

The illustration to the right (see Figure 63) will give you an idea of some of the defects found in dimensional lumber. Typical defects are checks that result from separation of wood across annual rings, knots that result from a portion of a tree branch incorporated in cut lumber, and splits which are a separation of the wood due to tearing apart of wood cells. A shake is a lengthwise separation of the wood which usually occurs between the rings of annual growth. None of the above defects should cause you to reject lumber outright. However, wood with a bow, cup, crook, wane, split or twist should be avoided in building construction. Dimensional lumber is typically sold in incremental lengths of 2 feet – for example, 2x6 lumber comes in lengths of 8, 10, 12, 14, 16, and 20 feet. When you plan your storage building, you should try to consider standard board lengths in the overall dimensions of your storage building. A 12' x 16' storage building (192 sq. ft.) will be far more economical to build than a storage building measuring 11' x 19' (209 sq. ft.) due to wastage.

The chart below shows you how many studs to purchase for a given length of wall. You should add 2 studs for each corner and 2 extra studs for each door and window.

For example, a 2x6 board measures approximately 1-1/2" x 5-1/2" depending upon moisture content and surface. Lumber that has a rough surface will measure close to the nominal size in comparison to lumber that is surfaced on four sides (known as S4S).

The most critical factor in determining the actual sizes of dimensional lumber is the moisture content of the wood. Look for the grade stamp imprinted on lumber to determine moisture content. Typical moisture content ratings are:

MC 15 (less than 15% moisture content)
S-DRY (less than 19% moisture content)
S-GRN (greater than 19% moisture content)

A 2x6 surfaced unseasoned board (S-GRN) will actually measure 1-9/16" x 5-5/8" compared to 1-1/2" x 5-1/2" for a 2x6 rated surfaced dry (S-DRY). The chart at right shows actual versus nominal sizes of dimensional lumber which is S4S and S-DRY or better. Avoid unseasoned lumber especially in the framing of your storage building. Lumber which is unseasoned can shrink considerably as it dries naturally and is certain to cause structural problems as your storage building ages.

Figure 63 - Lumber Defects

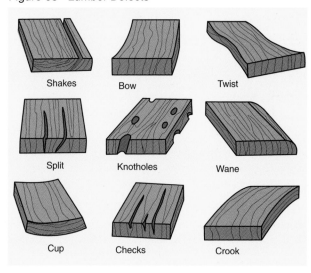

Standard Dimensions of Surfaced Lumber

Nominal Size	Surfaced (Actual) Size
1 x 2	3/4" x 1-1/2"
1 x 3	3/4" x 2-1/2"
1 x 4	3/4" x 3-1/2"
1 x 6	3/4" x 5-1/2"
1 x 8	3/4" x 7-1/4"
1 x 10	3/4" x 9-1/4"
1 x 12	3/4" x 11-1/4"
2 x 3	1-1/2" x 2-1/2"
2 x 4	1-1/2" x 3-1/2"
2 x 6	1-1/2" x 5-1/2"
2 x 8	1-1/2" x 7-1/4"
2 x 10	1-1/2" x 9-1/4"
2 x 12	1-1/2" x 11-1/4"
4 x 4	3-1/2" x 3-1/2"
4 x 10	3-1/2" x 9-1/4"
6 x 8	5-1/2" x 7-1/2"

Studs Required for Length of Wall

Studs Required for Walls:	Wall Length (in feet)													
	2	3	4	5	6	8	9	10	11	12	14	16	20
16" on center	2	3	4	5	6	6	7	8	9	9	12	13	16
24" on center	2	3	3	4	4	5	5	6	7	7	8	9	11

Choosing the correct lumber for your storage building can be as consequential as determining the correct design. For use in a storage building, the lumber you select must perform well in an exposed outdoor environment. Performance is measured according to the following criteria:

Freedom from Shrinkage and Warping - Lumber that has dimensional stability will not cause problems later.

Decay Resistance - Generally lumber cut from the heartwood (center of the log) is more resistant to decay than lumber cut from sapwood (outside of the log). However, chemical pressure-treatment can provide decay resistance to species that lack this property.

Workability - Refers to the ease with which you can saw, nail, or shape lumber.

Nail Holding - Determines whether or not a given species possesses good nail-holding power.

Paint Holding - The ability to hold a finish. Some species which contain high levels of natural extractives (such as pitch or resins) do not hold a finish well.

Fire Resistance - All woods are combustible, but some resist fire better than others. Woods that do not contain large amounts of resin are relatively slow to ignite.

Strength and Weight - Wood that is relatively light in weight but possesses great strength is ideal.

While no single species performs ideally according to all of the criteria above, Menards will be able to advise you regarding the lumber species most suited to your area. Often you must balance considerations of economy with performance. For example, redwood is considered a premium construction material, but high transportation cost outside the area of manufacture make pressure-treated pine woods a more economical alternative.

Here is a concise guide to some common softwood lumber species used in storage building construction:

Cedar, Western Red - Popular for the durability and decay-resistance of its heartwood.

Cypress - Cypress resists decay, has an attractive reddish coloration, and holds paint well.

Douglas Fir, Larch - Douglas fir has great strength and is used best in the substructure of your deck, especially in the joist members.

Pines - Numerous pine species have excellent workability but must be pressure-treated for use in deck construction.

Southern Pine - Unlike the soft pines described above, southern pines possess strength but are only moderately decay and warp resistant.

Poplar - Has moderate strength, resists decay and warping.

Redwood - The premium decking material because of its durability, resistance to decay, and beautiful natural brownish-red coloration.

Remember that in certain circumstances you can use two different species of lumber to construct your storage building. For example, redwood can be used for exterior trim while douglas fir is used for strength in the storage building wall and roof framing.

Whatever lumber species you select, it is important to learn the difference between the grain patterns in dimensional lumber. Flat grain lumber is cut with the grain parallel to the face of the board. Typically used for decking, flat grain boards should be used with the bark-side up in order to minimize cupping and grain separation. Vertical grain lumber, a more expensive grade used for finish work, is cut with the grain perpendicular to the face of the board.

Using Engineered Lumber

Due to recent developments in timber cutting practices and the reduced availability of certain sizes of framing lumber, engineered lumber manufactured from plywood, wood chips, and special glue resins offers an attractive alternative to dimensional lumber used for joists, beams, headers, and rafters. Unlike sawn dimensional lumber, engineered lumber is a manufactured product that will not warp and shrink over time.

Engineered lumber is manufactured to meet stringent criteria for strength, uniformity, and reliability. Glu-lam beams offer great strength over spans. Wood I-beams provide a lightweight alternative to conventional rafters. Some typical laminated veneer lumber products are shown to the right.

Figure 65 - Engineered Lumber

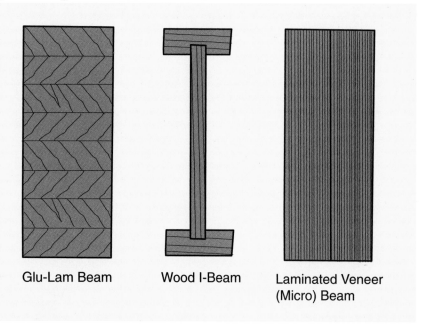

Glu-Lam Beam   Wood I-Beam   Laminated Veneer (Micro) Beam

ORDERING STORAGE BUILDING MATERIALS

Complete the sample material list on page 66 before you begin to shop. If you are using one of the storage building plans offered in the back of this manual, each plan comes with a complete list of materials. If you have designed your own storage building, create a material list from the final design after approval by your local building department.

Once you have completed the sample material list, visit the Menards Building Materials Desk to shop for your materials. Be aware that you will add to the cost of your project if you purchase your materials in a piecemeal fashion. Keep in mind that Menards offers quality materials and the level of service provided to make your storage building project even easier.

Especially consider the quality and grade of the lumber you are purchasing. Poor quality materials will yield a meager return on your storage building investment.

Don't hesitate to order at least a 5-10% overage of materials to make up for inevitable cutting mistakes or lumber defects. Be aware that dimensional lumber is sold either by the board foot, the lineal (or running) foot, or by the piece. A board foot of lumber represents the amount of lumber in a board 1" thick x 12' wide x 12' long. Use the following formula to compute board feet:

$$\text{Board Feet} = \frac{\text{Length (Feet) x Width (Inches) x Thickness (Inches)}}{12}$$

SAMPLE MATERIALS LIST

	Size	Length	Quantity X	Cost =	Total Cost
Foundation					
Concrete					
Sand					
Gravel					
Substructure					
Girders					
Skids					
Floor Joists					
Rim Joists					
4' x 8'-3/4" CDX Plywood					
Wall Framing					
Bottom Plates					
Cripple Studs					
Wall Studs					
Top and Tie Plates					
Headers Over Doors					
Headers Over Windows					
Roofing & Siding					
Rafters					
Collar Ties					
Fly Rafters					
Ridge Board					
4' x 8'-1/2" Roof Sheathing					
Roofing Felt					
Self-Sealing Shingles					
4' x 8'-1/2" T1-11 Siding					
Windows & Doors					
Windows					
Doors					
Connectors					
Nails					
Screws					
Bottom Plate to Stud Ties					
Tie Plate to Rafter Ties					
Grand Total					

Nails are the most common fastener used in storage building framing and construction. Nail lengths are indicated by the term penny, noted by a small letter **d**. In most cases, nails increase in diameter as they increase in length. Heavier construction framing is accomplished with common nails. The extra thick shank of the common nail has greater strength than other types. A wide thick head spreads the load and resists pull-through. For the substructure and framing of your storage building where nails are hidden, consider vinyl coated sinkers or cement coated nails which bond to the wood and will not pull up as readily as uncoated nails.

Box nails are similar in shape to common nails, but they have a slimmer shank that is less likely to split wood. Finishing nails are used in work where you want to counter sink and then cover the nail head.

Roofing nails are essential for attaching roofing materials and preventing moisture penetration through the nail hole.

Screws create neat, strong joists for finished work. Heavy-duty lag screws and lag bolts are useful for heavier framing connections, such as girder-to-post.

Discuss your project with your local Menards Building Materials Desk associate to determine the best nail and fastener selections for your storage building project.

Figure 67 - Nails and Fasteners

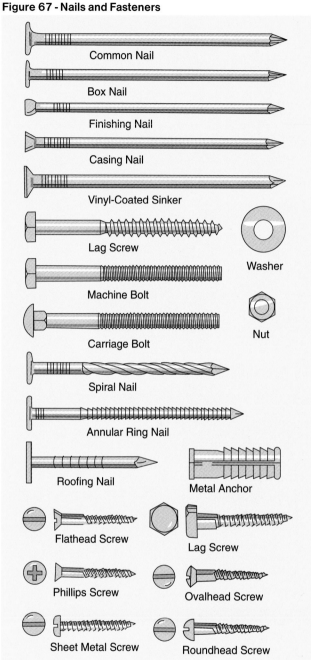

Common Nail
Box Nail
Finishing Nail
Casing Nail
Vinyl-Coated Sinker
Lag Screw
Washer
Machine Bolt
Carriage Bolt
Nut
Spiral Nail
Annular Ring Nail
Roofing Nail
Metal Anchor
Flathead Screw
Lag Screw
Phillips Screw
Ovalhead Screw
Sheet Metal Screw
Roundhead Screw

Table of Common Nails

Size	Length	Gauge	# per lb.
2d	1"	15	840
3d	1 1/4"	14	540
4d	1 1/2"	12 1/2	290
5d	1 3/4"	12 1/2	250
6d	2"	11 1/2	160
7d	2 1/4"	11 1/2	150
8d	2 1/2"	10 1/4	100
9d	2 3/4"	10 1/4	90
10d	3"	9	65
12d	3 1/4"	9	60
16d	3 1/2"	8	45
20d	4"	6	30
30d	4 1/2"	5	20
40d	5"	4	16
50d	5 1/2"	3	12
60d	6"	2	10

Finishing Nail Selection Chart

Size	Length	Gauge	# per lb.
2d	1"	16	1000
3d	1 1/4"	15 1/2	870
4d	1 1/2"	15	600
6d	2"	13	310
8d	2 1/2"	12 1/2	190
10d	3"	11 1/2	120

These tables show the approximate number of nails you get in a pound. You'll need more pounds of larger sizes to do a job. For outside jobs, get galvanized or cadmium-plated nails. Aluminum nails are a bit more expensive unless you are doing a smaller project.

Screw Selection Chart

Size	Length	Size	Length
0	1/4-3/8	9	1/2-3
1	1/4-1/2	10	1/2-31/2
2	1/4-3/4	11	5/8-31/2
3	1/4-1	12	5/8-4
4	1/4-11/2	14	3/4-5
5	3/8-11/2	16	1-5
6	3/8-21/2	18	1 1/4-5
7	3/8-21/2	20	1 1/2-5
8	3/8-3	24	3-5

The screw chart shows sizes and the lengths in which they're available. The larger sizes come in longer lengths. Most jobs call for sizes 6-12 in 1/2 to 3 inch lengths. Check size & length before you buy.

FRAMING WITH METAL FASTENERS

A wide variety of metal fasteners are available to make your storage building sturdy and long-lasting. You may be required by local codes to add seismic and hurricane connectors to each stud where it connects to the bottom and top plate. Rafter and tie plate connectors offer a quick method of attaching the roof rafters to the tie plate without making a bird's mouth cut. Nail-on plates can replace plywood gussets in gambrel roof construction and help to create a rigid roof frame. Be sure to follow the manufacturer's installation instructions.

Figure 68 - Variety of Metal Fasteners

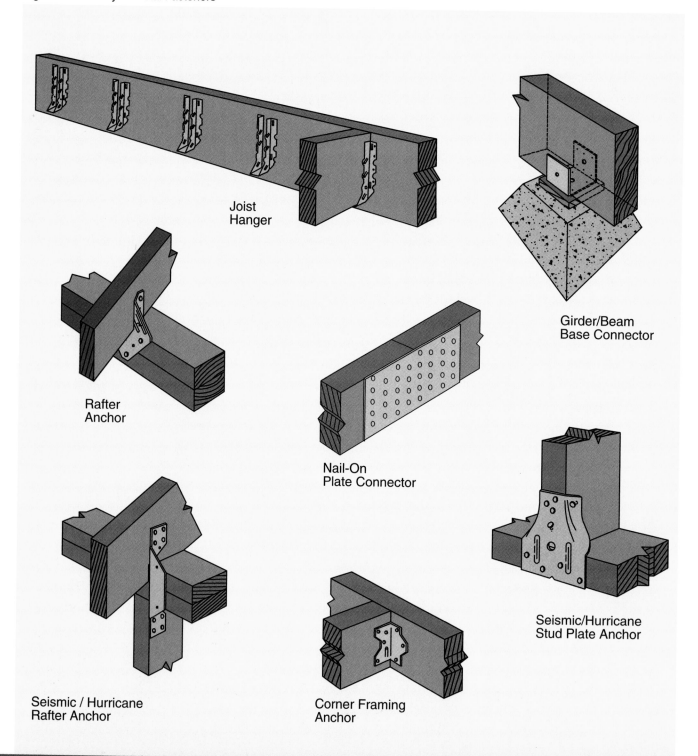

Joist Hanger

Girder/Beam Base Connector

Rafter Anchor

Nail-On Plate Connector

Seismic/Hurricane Stud Plate Anchor

Seismic / Hurricane Rafter Anchor

Corner Framing Anchor

Right-angled corner framing anchors add strength to perpendicular butt joints, especially where rim joists meet. Use joist hangers to attach your floor joists to rim joist members. Beam connectors provide a strong connection between beams and posts or pier blocks. The modest additional expense of metal fasteners will be more than offset by the added durability of your storage building. Secure fasteners using the short ribbed nails provided or where extra strength is required use lag screws in addition to nails.

Figure 69A - Girder/Beam Frame Connector

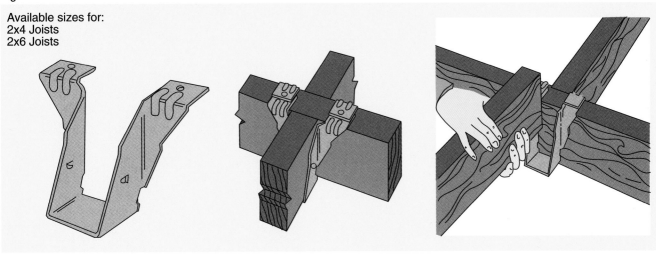

Available sizes for:
2x4 Joists
2x6 Joists

Figure 69B - Variety of Connectors

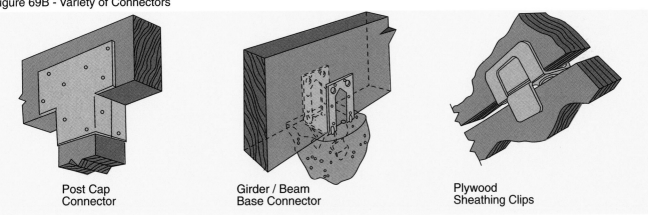

Post Cap
Connector

Girder / Beam
Base Connector

Plywood
Sheathing Clips

Figure 69C - Adjustable Post Anchor

Available sizes for:
4x4 Posts
4x6 Posts
6x6 Posts

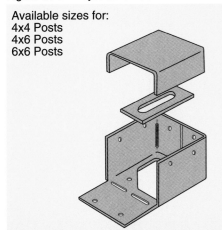
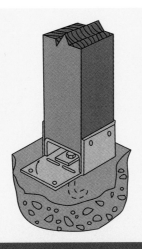

Floor Framing Plan

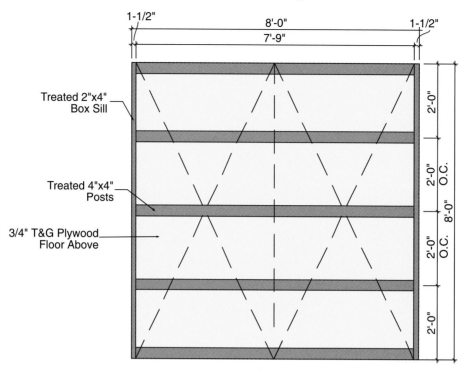

Treated 2"x4" Box Sill

Treated 4"x4" Posts

3/4" T&G Plywood Floor Above

1-1/2" 8'-0" 1-1/2"
7'-9"

2'-0" 2'-0" 2'-0" 2'-0" O.C. 8'-0"

Floor Plan

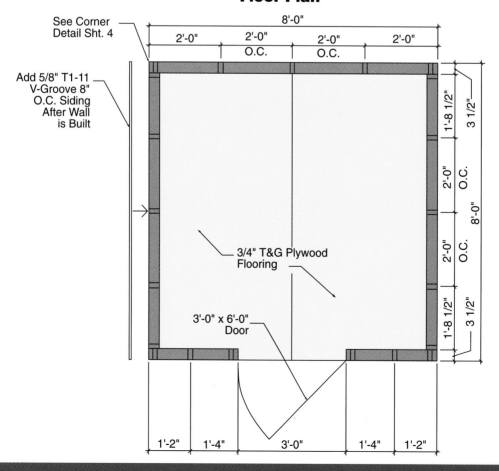

See Corner Detail Sht. 4

Add 5/8" T1-11 V-Groove 8" O.C. Siding After Wall is Built

3/4" T&G Plywood Flooring

3'-0" x 6'-0" Door

8'-0"
2'-0" 2'-0" 2'-0" 2'-0"
O.C. O.C.

1'-8 1/2" 3 1/2"
2'-0" O.C. 8'-0"
2'-0" O.C.
1'-8 1/2" 3 1/2"

1'-2" 1'-4" 3'-0" 1'-4" 1'-2"

Rear Wall Framing Plan

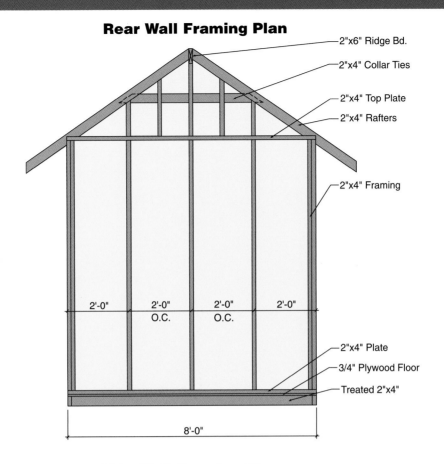

- 2"x6" Ridge Bd.
- 2"x4" Collar Ties
- 2"x4" Top Plate
- 2"x4" Rafters
- 2"x4" Framing
- 2"x4" Plate
- 3/4" Plywood Floor
- Treated 2"x4"

2'-0"   2'-0" O.C.   2'-0" O.C.   2'-0"

8'-0"

Side Wall Framing Plan

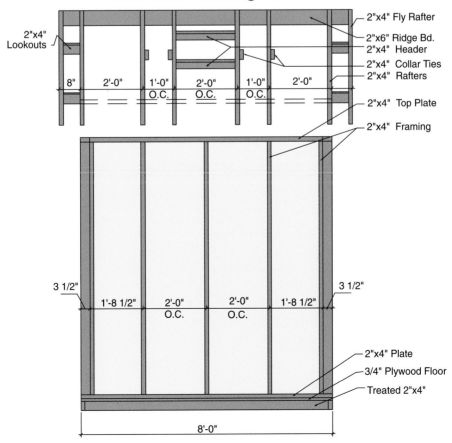

- 2"x4" Fly Rafter
- 2"x6" Ridge Bd.
- 2"x4" Header
- 2"x4" Collar Ties
- 2"x4" Rafters
- 2"x4" Top Plate
- 2"x4" Framing
- 2"x4" Lookouts

8"   2'-0"   1'-0" O.C.   2'-0" O.C.   1'-0" O.C.   2'-0"

- 2"x4" Plate
- 3/4" Plywood Floor
- Treated 2"x4"

3 1/2"   1'-8 1/2"   2'-0" O.C.   2'-0" O.C.   1'-8 1/2"   3 1/2"

8'-0"

To begin, cut both the top and bottom plates to length. In most cases, you will need more than one piece of lumber for each plate. So locate the joints at stud centers and offset joints between top and bottom plates by at least 4'-0" (see Figure 72).

Lay the top plate against the bottom plate on the floor as illustrated below. Beginning at one end, measure 15-1/4" in and draw a line across both plates. Measure out farther along the plates an additional distance of 1-1/2" from this line, and draw a second line. The first interior stud will be placed between these lines. From these lines, advance 16" at a time, drawing new lines, until you reach the far end of the plates. Each set of lines will outline the placement of a stud with all studs evenly spaced at 16" on center. If you are using studs on 24" centers, the first measurement in from the edge would be 23-1/4".

Assembling the Pieces

If you are using precut studs (either 92-1/4" or 92-5/8" in length), no cutting is required. Otherwise measure and cut the wall studs to exact length. Position the plates apart on the floor and turn them on edge with the stud marking toward the center. Place the studs between the lines and nail them through each plate with two 16d common nails.

Framing Corners

Where walls meet, you might need extra studs to handle the corner tie to the adjacent wall. These extra studs should be added to the ends of the longer two of the four walls. The exact positioning of these extra corner studs is shown at the bottom of page 76.

Figure 72 - Assembling the Wall Frame

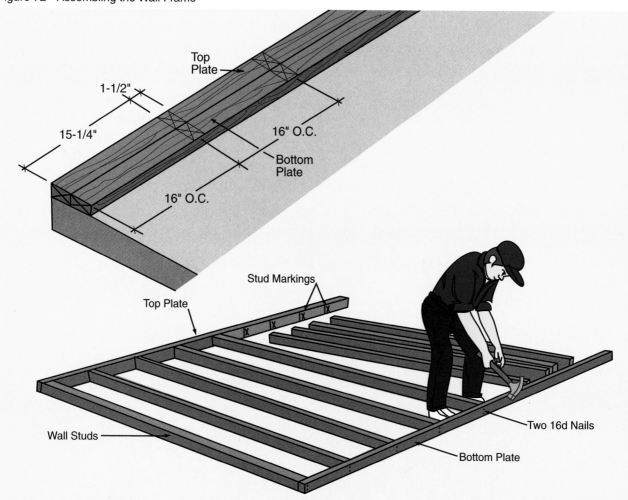

At door and window openings there is no stud support, so a header is required. Door and window headers can be constructed either from 4x dimensional lumber, veneer laminate lumber also known as engineered lumber, or two lengths of 2x material on edge with a 1/2" piece of plywood sandwiched between them. When you are constructing a built-up header from doubled-up 2x material, the plywood makes the header the same 3-1/2" width as the studs.

Headers are always installed on edge as shown. Consult the chart at right to determine the header size required for a given span.

The spaces above door openings and above and below windows are framed with cripple studs spaced 16" on center. Study the illustrations to become familiar with the king and trimmer stud locations used in framing doors and windows.

The rough framed door should be 1-1/2" higher than the usual 80" actual door height and 2-1/2" wider than the door to account for doorjamb material. When the 1-1/2" bottom plate is cut from the opening, this adds the needed 1-1/2" in extra height.

In addition to cripple studs, king studs, and trimmer studs, window framing also uses a rough sill to support the window. Headers should be set at the same time as door headers. Consult the manufacturer's instructions for a suggested rough-out opening to accommodate a given window.

Header Size (4x or built-up 2x)	Maximum Span (feet)
4 x 4	4'
4 x 6	6'
4 x 8	8'
4 x 10	10'
4 x 12	12'

Header Assembly

Nail two pieces of 2xs and plywood to the length between king studs with 16d nails spaced 16" apart along both top and bottom edges.

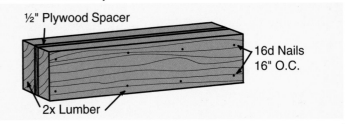

Figure 73A - Header Assembly

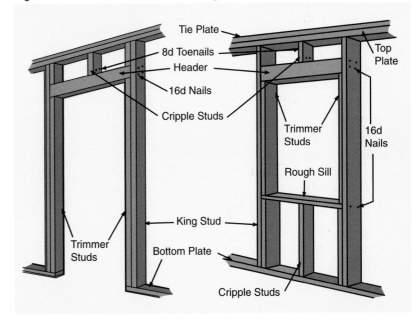

Figure 73B - Door and Window Framing

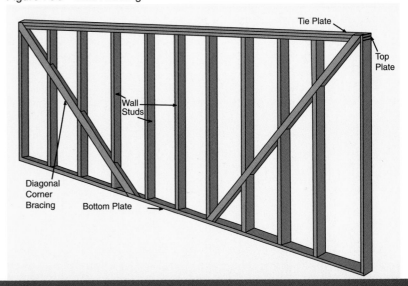

Figure 73C - Wall Framing

Structures with plywood siding normally do not require bracing, but all others do. The two most commonly used types of bracing are wooden "let-in" bracing made of 1x4 stock and metal strap bracing.

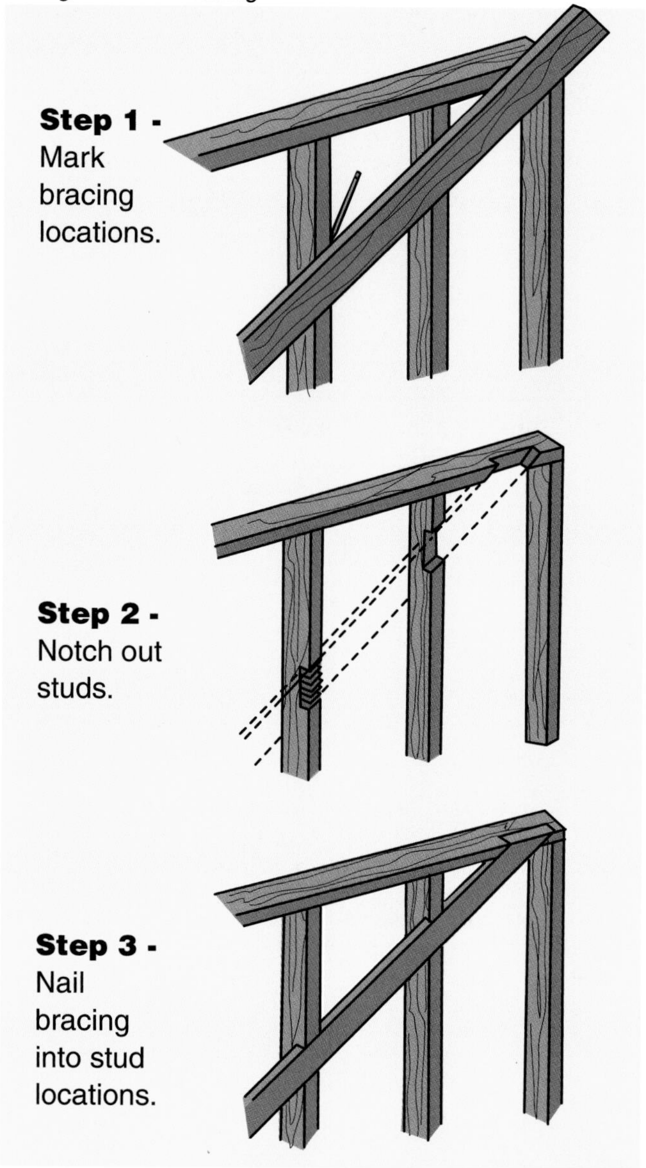

Let-in Bracing

This type of wooden bracing runs from the top outside corners of the wall to the bottom center of the wall. It forms a V-shaped configuration as shown on page 73. These braces are set into notched studs and are prepared while the wall frame is still lying on the slab.

Lay the 1x4 on the frame with one end at a top corner and the other end as far out on the bottom plate as possible without running into any door or window opening. Mark the underside of the brace where it overhangs the top and bottom plates to determine the angle at which the plates cross. Also mark both sides of the studs and plates at each point the brace crosses them. Notch the studs at these locations by making repeated cuts with your circular saw. Use a hammer and wood chisel to knock out any stubborn chips. Trim the ends of the 1x4 and put the brace in place. Hold it in place with a single nail until the wall is raised and plumbed. Then nail the brace fast with 8d nails wherever it crosses a plate or stud.

Metal Strap Bracing

Commonly available in 10' to 12' lengths, this type of bracing is nailed to the outside of the studded walls after they are raised, square, and plumb. Metal bracing is thin enough not to obstruct the exterior wall sheathing.

The straps have predrilled holes every 2" sized to accept an 8d nail. Strap bracing must always be installed in crossed pairs, similar to a large X design.

Figure 74A - Bracing

Step 1 - Mark bracing locations.

Step 2 - Notch out studs.

Step 3 - Nail bracing into stud locations.

Figure 74B - Alternative Metal Strap

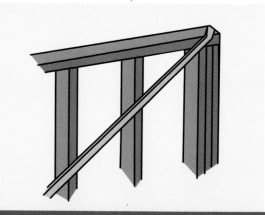

Most walls can be raised by hand if enough help is available on the job site. It is advisable to have one person for every 10' of wall for the lifting operation.

The order in which walls are framed and raised can vary from job to job, but in general, the longer exterior walls are framed first. The shorter exterior walls are then raised and the corners are nailed together.

Once the first wall is framed out, there are only a few short steps until it is up and standing. If you are raising a wall on a slab, slide the wall along the slab until the bottom plate lies near the anchor bolt at the floor's edge. If you are raising a wall on a wood floor, you might want to tack some scrap lumber along the floor rim joists to prevent the wall from slipping over the edge. To raise the wall, you should have your workers grip it at the top plate in unison and work their hands beneath the plate. Now everyone walks down the wall until it is in the upright position. On a slab you need to slip the bottom plate in place over the anchor bolts as you tilt the wall up.

To brace the wall, tack 2x4 braces to the wall studs, one at each end and one in the middle if the wall is particularly long. Tie these braces into stakes driven firmly into the ground or tack them to the wood floor rim joists if appropriate. Secure the wall by using washers and nuts if you have anchor bolts or tack the bottom plate to the wood floor. Do not securely nail the bottom plate to the floor until you are certain that the wall is in proper alignment.

To check alignment, use a carpenter's level to check the wall for plumb along both end studs on adjacent faces. If the wall is out of plumb, loosen that brace, align the wall, and secure the brace again. If an end stud is warped, bridge the warp with a straight board. When both ends are plumb, adjust the middle.

Figure 75 - To raise the wall, have your workers grip it at the top plate in unison and work their hands beneath the plate. Now everyone walks until it is in the upright position.

To check alignment, use a carpenter's level.

Nailing Schedule for Structural Members

Description of Building Materials	Number & Type of Fastener	Spacing of Fasteners
Top or sole plate to stud, end nail	2-16d	-
Stud to sole plate, toenail	4-8d or 3-16d	-
Doubled studs, face nail	16d	24" O.C.
Doubled top plates, face nail	16d	16" O.C.
Top plates, taps and intersections, face nail	2-16d	-
Continued header, two pieces	16d	16" O.C. along each edge
Ceiling joists to plate, toenail	2-16d	-
Continuous header to stud, toenail	4-8d	-
Ceiling joist, taps over partitions, face nail	3-16d	-
Ceiling joist to parallel rafters, face nail	3-16d	-
Rafter to plate, toenail	2-16d	-
1" brace to each stud and plate, face nail	2-8d	-
Built-up corner studs	16d	30" O.C.
Built-up girder and beams	16d	32" O.C. at top & bottom & staggered 2-20d at ends & at each splice
Roof rafters to ridge, valley or hip rafters, toenail	4-16d	-
Face nail	3-16d	-
Collar ties to rafters, face nail	3-8d	-
Description of Building Materials	Description of Fasteners	Spacing of Fasteners
Roof and wall sheathing to frame		
1/2 inch to 5/16 inch Roof & Wall sheathing to frame	6d	6" edges 12" intermediate supports
Other wall sheathing		
1/2 inch Fiberboard sheathing	1 1/2" galvanized roofing nail 6d common nail	3" edges 6" intermediate supports

Once raised, the wall should also be checked for levelness. If needed, it can be shimmed level using tapered cedar shingles driven between the foundation and the bottom plate. Once the wall is plumb and level, tighten the anchor nuts to their final tightness or on wooden floors nail two 16d common nails between each stud. Do not nail the bottom plate in a door opening since this section must be cut out for the door.

At corners, nail through the end walls into the stud using 16d common nails staggered every 12". When the walls are up, you can then add the 2x4 tie plates to the top plates on each wall. These tie plates lap over onto adjacent walls to interlock the walls and give added strength to the structure.

Figure 76A - Corner Detail From Above

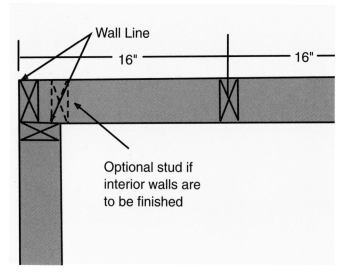

Wall Line

16" 16"

Optional stud if interior walls are to be finished

Figure 76B - Leveling Wall

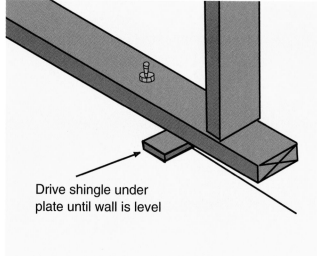

Drive shingle under plate until wall is level

Figure 76C - Corner Detail From Side

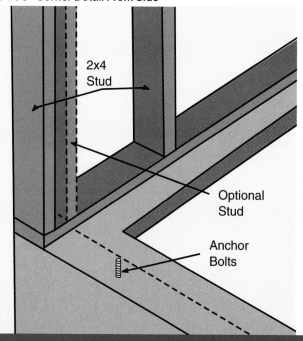

2x4 Stud

Optional Stud

Anchor Bolts

Figure 76D - Corner Detail Top Plates

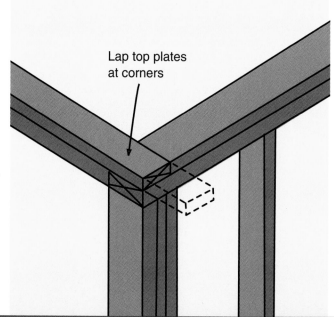

Lap top plates at corners

Most roof designs are variations of the gable roof, in which evenly spaced pairs of common rafters join the tie plates and central ridge board together. A hip roof is also used in storage building construction and most often utilizes small hip roof trusses to create the roof framing. Rafters are 2x4s, 2x6s, or 2x8s depending upon span, spacing, load, and roof slope. They are installed on 16" or 24" centers. Check with your local building department for help regarding rafter requirements and roof load in your area. At the peak, rafter boards butt against a central ridge board. The ridge board can be either 1x or 2x lumber and is one size wider than the rafter lumber. Slope, or pitch, is referred to in terms of unit rise in a given unit run. Unit run is fixed at 12 inches. Unit rise is the slope over those 12 inches. A rise of 4" over 12" equals a slope of "4 in 12".

Cutting the Rafters

A common rafter has three cuts: the plumb cut to form the angle where the rafter meets the ridge board, the bird's mouth notch to fit the top plate, and the tail cut at the end of the overhang. Professionally prepared plans often have a template or diagram that serves as a master for rafter cutting. Cut two rafters off the master and check them for accuracy before using the others. Use a steel carpenter's square to mark the cuts.

Raising the Roof

With ridge board and rafters cut, you can raise the roof. Unless the roof is small, you'll need three people. Nail an upright 2x4 for each of the end rafters flush against the middle of the end top plate. One person then lines up one end rafter with the end of the side top plate and ties it in with three 16d nails. The second raises and holds it at the correct slope against one of the 2x4s, while the third tacks the two together. Do the same with the opposite end rafter, then align the ridge board between the top of the rafters and tie it in with three 16d common nails through each rafter. Use 8d common nails if the ridge board is 1x common lumber. The ridge board must be level, and the rafter ends must be flush with the sides of the ridge board. Repeat the process at the opposite end for a single-piece ridge board. For a two-piece ridge board, connect the rafters to the last spacing mark at the opposite end.

Figure 77 - For those of us not familiar with a square, lay out the initial pair of rafters on the slab. Snap chalk lines to represent the bottom of the rafters and the plate line. Use the rise in 12" to establish the angle (for example, 4" in 12"). If they fit, use them as patterns for all other rafters.

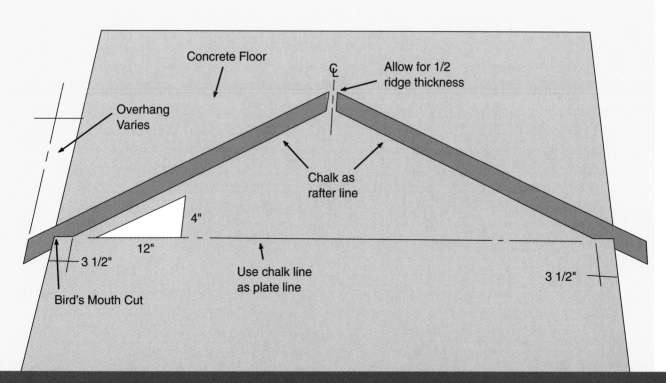

Figure 78A - Typical Storage Building Section
(for reference only)

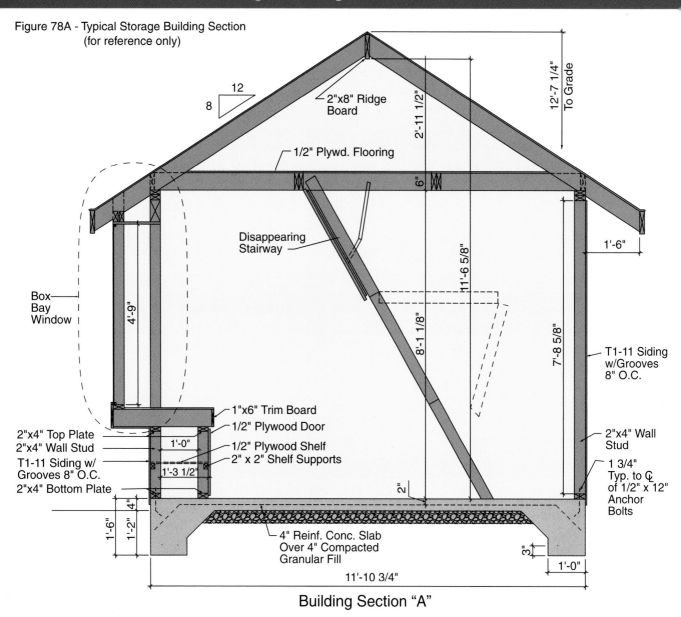

Building Section "A"

Labels in figure:
- 12 / 8 (slope triangle)
- 2"x8" Ridge Board
- 1/2" Plywd. Flooring
- 12'-7 1/4" To Grade
- 2'-11 1/2"
- 6"
- 1'-6"
- Disappearing Stairway
- 11'-6 5/8"
- 7'-8 5/8"
- 8'-1 1/8"
- Box Bay Window
- 4'-9"
- T1-11 Siding w/Grooves 8" O.C.
- 1"x6" Trim Board
- 1/2" Plywood Door
- 1/2" Plywood Shelf
- 2" x 2" Shelf Supports
- 2"x4" Top Plate
- 2"x4" Wall Stud
- T1-11 Siding w/ Grooves 8" O.C.
- 2"x4" Bottom Plate
- 1'-0"
- 1'-3 1/2"
- 2"x4" Wall Stud
- 1 3/4" Typ. to C of 1/2" x 12" Anchor Bolts
- 2"
- 1'-6"
- 1'-2"
- 4"
- 4" Reinf. Conc. Slab Over 4" Compacted Granular Fill
- 3"
- 1'-0"
- 11'-10 3/4"

Figure 78B - Typical Rafter Cutting Diagram

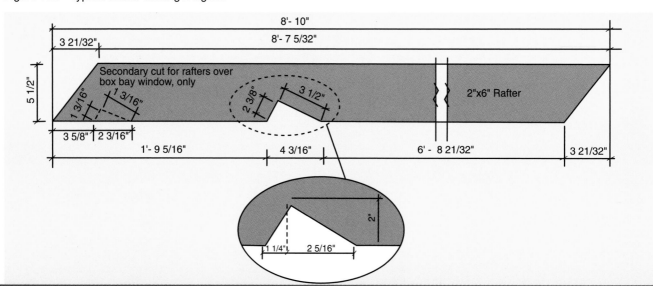

Labels in figure:
- 8'- 10"
- 8'- 7 5/32"
- 3 21/32"
- 5 1/2"
- Secondary cut for rafters over box bay window, only
- 1 3/16"
- 1 3/16"
- 2 3/8"
- 3 1/2"
- 2"x6" Rafter
- 3 5/8"
- 2 3/16"
- 1'- 9 5/16"
- 4 3/16"
- 6'- 8 21/32"
- 3 21/32"
- 2"
- 1 1/4"
- 2 5/16"

ROOF FRAMING (cont.)

Erecting the Rafters

Make sure the end rafters are plumb and that the ridge board is level and centered mid-span. Next attach a diagonal brace between the ridge board and the 2x4 nailed to the top plate. Run the remaining rafters in pairs, attaching them to the ridge board first, then to the top plate (see Figures 80A - B). If your local codes require seismic/hurricane anchors, use metal connectors to secure the rafters to the top plate.

If a second ridge board is used, the process is repeated from the opposite end of the building. The junction of the ridge boards must be covered by two rafters. If you plan to install rafter ties (or ceiling joists), use three 16d nails to tie rafters to the rafter ties and cut the ties to match the slope of the rafters.

Be sure to add collar ties and hangers before removing any shoring or bracing.

Figure 80A - Ridge Board Supports

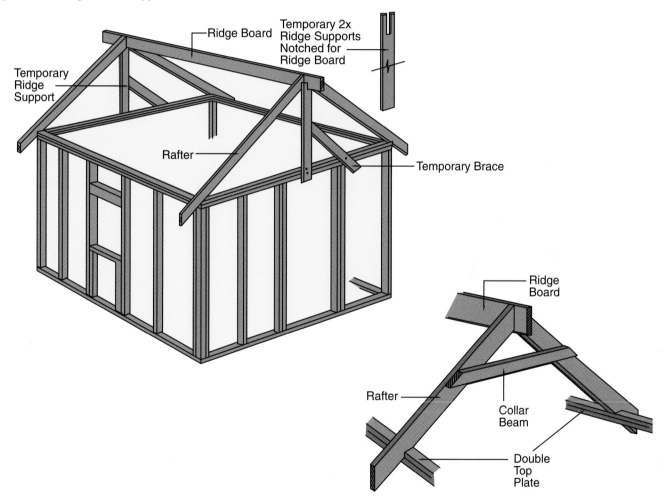

Figure 80B - Rafter Cuts

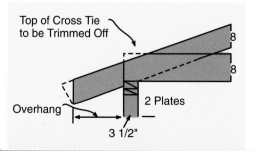

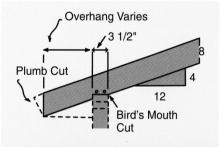

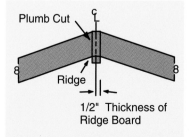

Using Metal Connectors For Framing

As mentioned earlier, metal fasteners provide the strength nails alone cannot provide. They also avoid the irritation of watching angled nails split the lumber that you have so carefully cut and fitted. Certain metal connectors allow the rafter to rest directly on the tie or top plate and eliminate the difficult and time-consuming bird's mouth cut.

Other connectors are designed to join the rafter to the ridge board without toenailing. As you can see from the illustrations below, many different types of metal connectors are available for roof framing work. While metal roof framing connectors will add some additional expense to your project, they will save you time and create a more durable storage building.

Figure 79 - Rafter Connector Examples

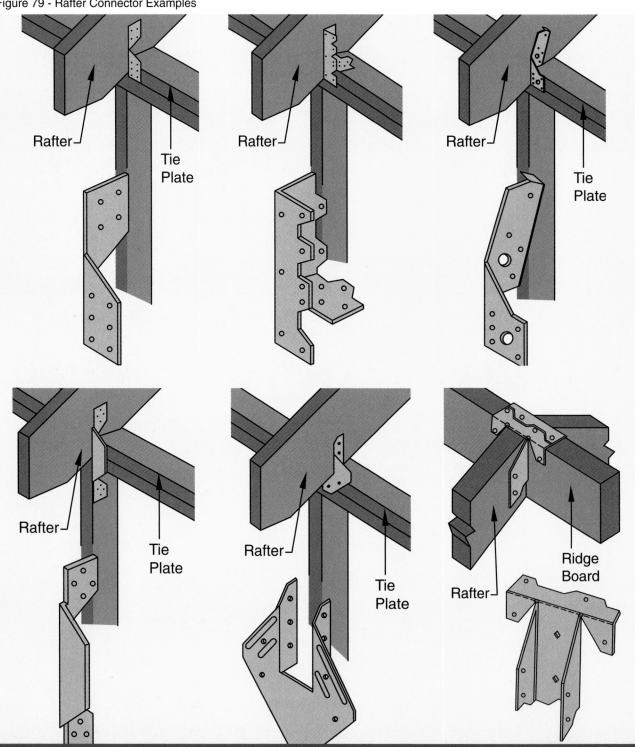

Variations of the Roof Cornice

Whatever type of roof you decide to construct, your building will have a roof overhang to protect the top of the side walls from moisture penetration. This overhang is generally known as the roof cornice. The cornice can also serve to provide ventilation and protection from the hot overhead rays of the sun on the sidewalls. As a general rule of thumb, warmer climates tend to favor longer overhangs that offer greater shading.

An open cornice is illustrated in Figure 81A. The overhang can extend up to 24" from the edge of the building. You have the option of adding a frieze board to the rafter ends or leaving the rafter ends exposed. Remember that when you create an exposed overhang, the roof sheathing is visible from underneath. Painting or staining the sheathing can improve its appearance.

Figure 81B represents a closed cornice. Make a seat cut on the rafter at the top plate. Cut the rafter ends flush and vertical with the top plate. Bring the siding all the way up to the rafters and finish off the cornice with a trim piece that covers the slightly exposed roof sheathing.

Two variations of the boxed cornice are shown in Figures 81C and 81D. A fascia board at the rafter ends is essential for any style of boxed cornice. Figure 81C demonstrates the sloping soffit design where the rafters are used to directly attach the soffit board. Nail a 1x fascia to the square cut rafter ends. Another frieze board covers the end portion of the soffit where it meets the wall siding.

Figure 81D portrays the level soffit design that requires 2x4 horizontal lookouts facenailed at the rafter ends and toenailed to wall siding. Level soffits generally extend no more than 12"-15" from the building wall. The lookouts help to frame the soffit construction.

Proper ventilation is essential for the boxed cornice. Install soffit vents (typically 4"x8") at regular intervals along the soffit between the lookouts. Be sure to install the screened vents or you will have unintentionally created a birdhouse wherever you have an unscreened vent!

Ventilation

If you plan to use your storage building as a work area where you will spend longer periods of time, consider installing either gable end vents or roof vents. Vents help to reduce interior temperatures during the summer and to minimize condensation during the winter months. Gable end vents should be installed at both gable ends of your roof to promote cross-ventilation.

The number of roof vents you will install depends upon the cubic footage of your building. Simply create a box frame between roof rafters and install the vent according to the manufacturer's instructions. Don't forget to flash and then caulk the vent after you have installed the roof sheathing and shingles.

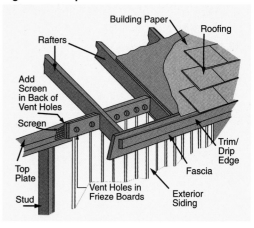

Figure 81A - Open Cornice

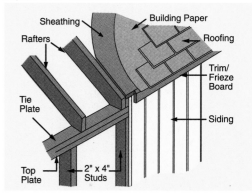

Figure 81B - Closed Cornice

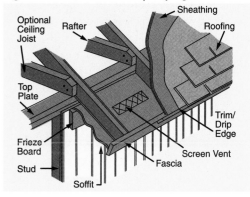

Figure 81C - Boxed Cornice/Sloping Soffit

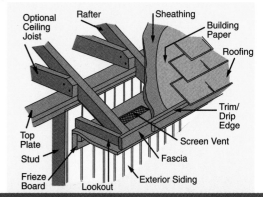

Figure 81D - Boxed Cornice/Level Soffit

Roof Sheathing

Use 4'x8' plywood roof sheathing panels to create a strong base for your roofing material. The required thickness of sheathing will vary with rafter spacing and local building code requirements. Generally, the wider the rafter spacing, the thicker the sheathing needs to be. If you want the interior of your storage building to have a finished building look, use 2x6 tongue and groove material to create a solid roof sheathing and paint the underside.

Stagger the sheathing, starting at the bottom, so that the end joints of adjacent sheets fall on different rafters. Space 6d nails 6" apart at sheet ends and 12" on center at intermediate rafters. Leave a 1/16" expansion gap between the ends of sheets. For larger jobs, you might want to rent a pneumatic staple gun to fasten sheathing. If gable eaves have an overhang, be certain to extend the sheathing to cover it.

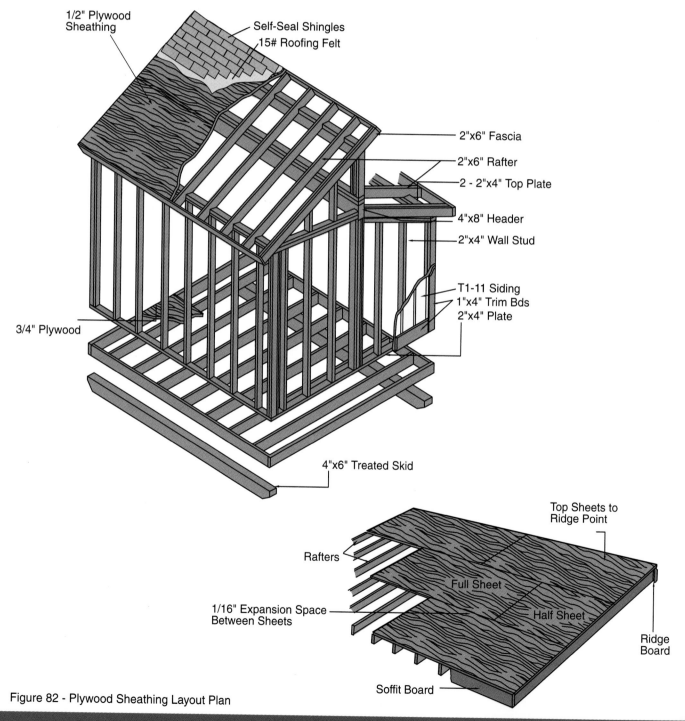

1/2" Plywood Sheathing

Self-Seal Shingles
15# Roofing Felt

2"x6" Fascia

2"x6" Rafter

2 - 2"x4" Top Plate

4"x8" Header

2"x4" Wall Stud

T1-11 Siding
1"x4" Trim Bds
2"x4" Plate

3/4" Plywood

4"x6" Treated Skid

Top Sheets to Ridge Point

Rafters

Full Sheet

Half Sheet

Ridge Board

1/16" Expansion Space Between Sheets

Soffit Board

Figure 82 - Plywood Sheathing Layout Plan

Gambrel Roof Construction

The gambrel roof offers an attractive barn-like alternative for storage building design. Construct gambrel roof framing from trusses built on the ground and then erect the relatively lightweight trusses over wall framing.

To add additional strength to your gambrel roof trusses in areas with heavy snow loads, use truss plate connectors and truss tie-down brackets to connect the truss to the top plate.

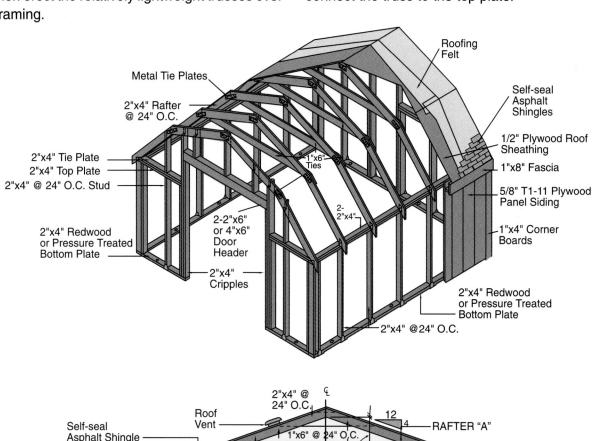

Metal Tie Plates

2"x4" Rafter @ 24" O.C.

2"x4" Tie Plate
2"x4" Top Plate
2"x4" @ 24" O.C. Stud

2"x4" Redwood or Pressure Treated Bottom Plate

1"x6" Ties

2-2"x6" or 4"x6" Door Header

2"x4" Cripples

2-2"x4"

2"x4" @ 24" O.C.

Roofing Felt

Self-seal Asphalt Shingles

1/2" Plywood Roof Sheathing

1"x8" Fascia

5/8" T1-11 Plywood Panel Siding

1"x4" Corner Boards

2"x4" Redwood or Pressure Treated Bottom Plate

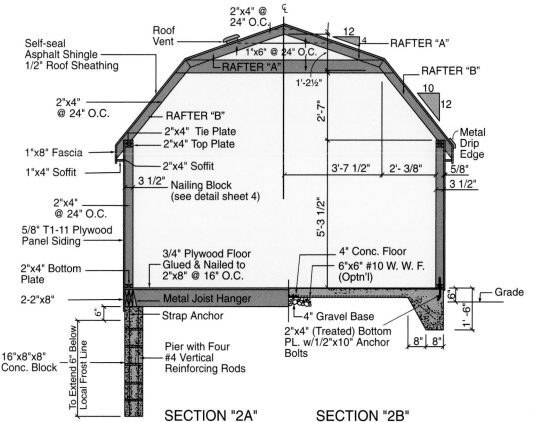

Self-seal Asphalt Shingle
1/2" Roof Sheathing

2"x4" @ 24" O.C.

Roof Vent

2"x4" @ 24" O.C.

1"x6" @ 24" O.C.

RAFTER "A"

RAFTER "A"

12
4

RAFTER "B"

RAFTER "B"

10
12

1'-2½"

2'-7"

3'-7 1/2"   2'- 3/8"

5/8"

Metal Drip Edge

3 1/2"

2"x4" Tie Plate
2"x4" Top Plate
2"x4" Soffit

1"x8" Fascia
1"x4" Soffit

3 1/2" Nailing Block (see detail sheet 4)

2"x4" @ 24" O.C.

5/8" T1-11 Plywood Panel Siding

2"x4" Bottom Plate

2-2"x8"

16"x8"x8" Conc. Block

To Extend 6" Below Local Frost Line

6"

5'-3 1/2"

3/4" Plywood Floor Glued & Nailed to 2"x8" @ 16" O.C.

Metal Joist Hanger

Strap Anchor

Pier with Four #4 Vertical Reinforcing Rods

4" Conc. Floor

6"x6" #10 W. W. F. (Optn'l)

2"x4" (Treated) Bottom PL. w/1/2"x10" Anchor Bolts

4" Gravel Base

Grade

6"

1'- 6"

8" 8"

SECTION "2A"   SECTION "2B"

Storage Building Roof Construction

The storage building roof lowers the height of one wall to create a lean-to appearance. Storage building roofing is typical for buildings with clerestory windows like the design illustrated below. The advantage of the storage building roof and clerestory window combination is that without wall windows all of your wall space is available for storage but you still have plenty of natural lighting provided by the windows above your workspace.

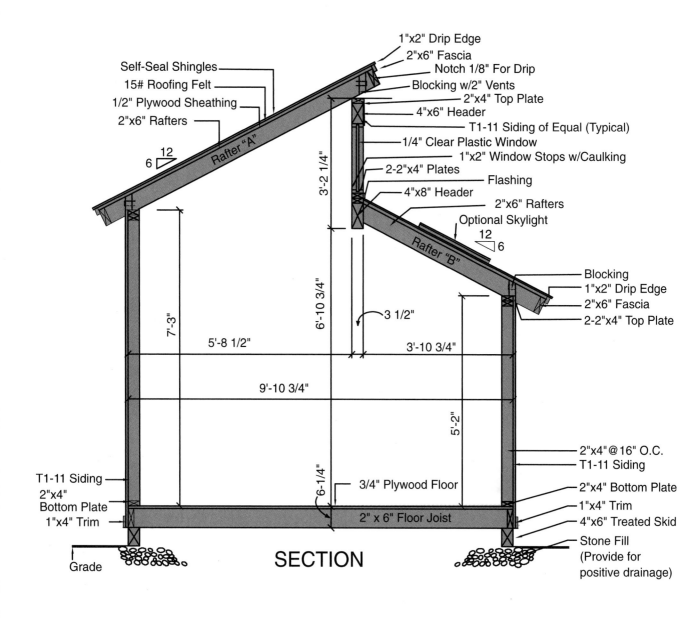

SECTION

Figure 84 - Section With Window Lighting

Before starting construction, select the siding and determine the need for wall sheathing. Wall sheathing requirements are determined by the stud spacing, the width of the door and window jambs, and the application of the trim (see Figure 85A).

A commonplace and inexpensive siding for storage buildings, T1-11 exterior siding does not require wall sheathing and adds structural strength. Flakeboard (Oriented Strand Board) is another inexpensive siding option for those with a tight budget. When you install vertical panel siding, nail 6d galvanized nails every 4"-6" at the edges of the panel and every 8"-12" inside the panel. You might be able to obtain siding nails that match the siding and thus eliminate painting both the siding and nails. If you have to add a panel above the bottom panel, use Z-bar flashing between the panels (see Figure 85C). Leave a 1/4" gap around door and window openings when cutting siding to facilitate fitting.

When plywood sheathing is used, diagonal corner bracing can often be omitted. Decide whether trim is to be applied on top of the siding or butted into it. If butted, apply trim first, then apply siding. Horizontal wood siding is more expensive than plywood panel siding but provides an attractive and durable exterior. However, horizontal wood siding requires periodic painting for preservation.

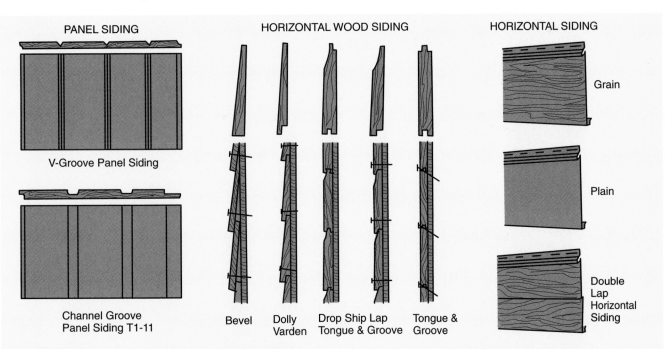

Figure 85A - Siding Alternatives

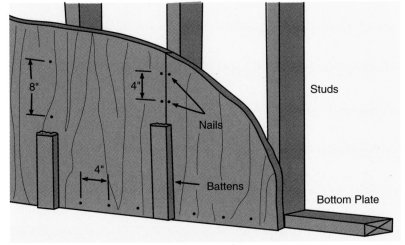

Figure 85B - Panel Siding With Batten Boards

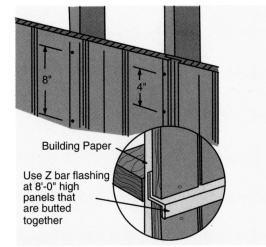

Figure 85C - Vertical Grooved Siding Panels

Lay down various lengths of siding at each side. Apply so that joints in the succeeding course do not fall directly above each other. Butt all joints over the center of a stud. Seal by painting the edges with primer before butting. Start the bottom of the first course 1/2" below the bottom plate. Siding on all walls should be aligned and level and each course equally spaced. Be especially careful to determine the lap and exposure to the weather before applying the second and succeeding courses. Measure the distance to be covered and divide it by the desired exposure to get the total number of courses of siding. See Figure 86A below. Carefully mark these spaces on the corners of each wall, taking into consideration the overlap of the siding. Run a chalk line from one mark to another, leaving a horizontal chalk line on the building paper as a guide. If you are not applying sheathing or building paper, chalk the wall studs directly. Apply the siding and keep it consistent by checking your level.

Final openings, where siding meets the soffit if applicable, can be closed with a piece of quarter round or shingle mould. Protect your storage building by painting or staining it as soon as possible.

Figure 86A - Marking Siding Courses

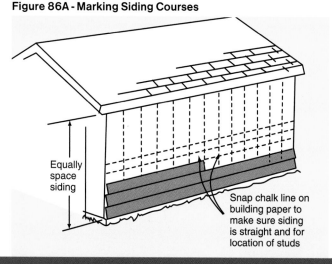

Equally space siding

Snap chalk line on building paper to make sure siding is straight and for location of studs

Figure 86B - Horizontal Siding Detail

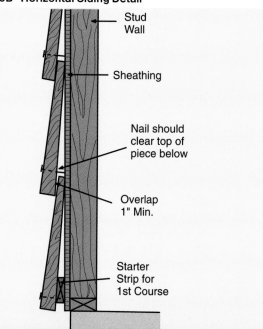

Stud Wall

Sheathing

Nail should clear top of piece below

Overlap 1" Min.

Starter Strip for 1st Course

BUILDING PAPER

Some local building codes might require that building paper be used to seal the wall from the elements. Building paper is typically felt or kraft paper impregnated with asphalt and is stapled or nailed between the siding and the sheathing or studs. Rolls are usually 36" wide and come in lengths covering between 200 to 500 square feet. Apply building paper in horizontal strips from the bottom of the wall as shown in Figure 86C. Overlaps should be 2" at horizontal joints, 6" at vertical joints, and 12" at corners. Cutting is done with a utility knife. Use just enough staples or nails in an installation to hold the paper in place. Siding nails will hold it permanently. Before you install siding, snap a level chalk line on the siding to indicate the bottom edge of the paper and work up.

Figure 86C - Applying Building Paper

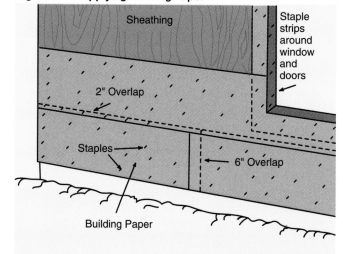

Sheathing

Staple strips around window and doors

2" Overlap

Staples

6" Overlap

Building Paper

Before applying trim, know the nailing requirements of the siding you select. Some siding will have trim applied over the siding, but other siding will butt against trim and require extra blocking at the edges. After the roof sheathing is on but before you install the fascia and rake boards, add soffit nailers if required. Use the longest fascia boards on the longest walls. Join all ends over the center of a rafter or nailer. Consult Figures 87A to 87F below. At the gable end, extend the fascia (or rake board) along the edge of the roof sheathing and rafter. At the top, cut the end to the angle of the rafter and butt at the center. Be sure to prime coat both ends before butting. At the lower end, let the front rake fascia extend beyond the side fascia, then cut the ends to line up with the side fascia.

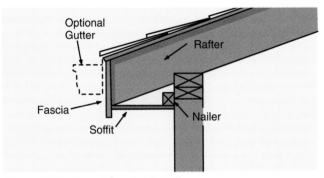

Figure 87A - Boxed Cornice Detail

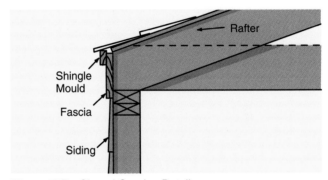

Figure 87B - Closed Cornice Detail

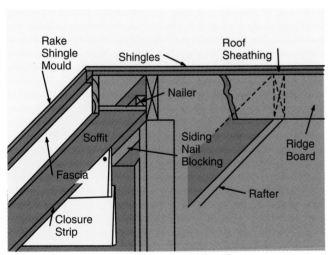

Figure 87C - Gable End Ridge Detail Box Overhang

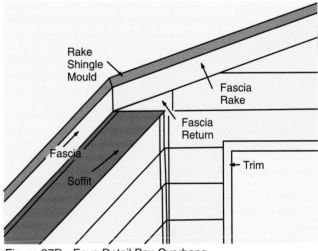

Figure 87D - Eave Detail Box Overhang

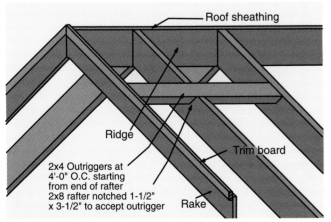

Figure 87E - Gable End Ridge Detail Open Overhang

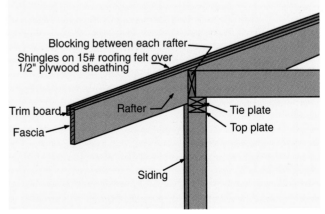

Figure 87F - Open Cornice Overhang

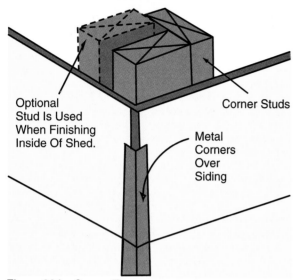

Optional
Stud Is Used
When Finishing
Inside Of Shed.

Corner Studs

Metal
Corners
Over
Siding

Figure 88A - Corner Tins

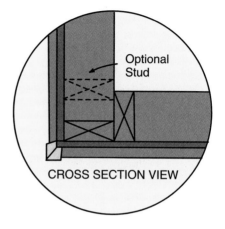

Optional
Stud

CROSS SECTION VIEW

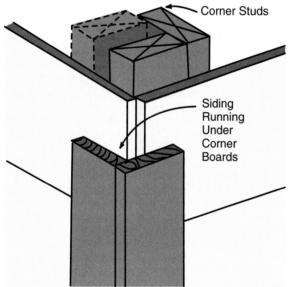

Corner Studs

Siding
Running
Under
Corner
Boards

Figure 88B - Corner Boards

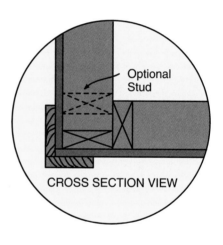

Optional
Stud

CROSS SECTION VIEW

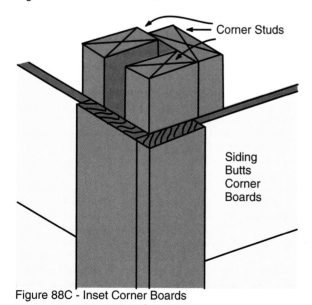

Corner Studs

Siding
Butts
Corner
Boards

Figure 88C - Inset Corner Boards

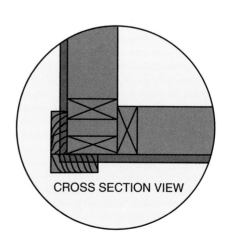

CROSS SECTION VIEW

WINDOW AND DOOR DETAILS

Study the typical window and door details shown in Figures 89A through 89D for examples of door and window framing construction. Because of the great variety in window manufacturing, it is best to study the window manufacturer's installation details before framing and trimming them. Small storage buildings can utilize a built on-site door constructed from plywood and 1x trim (see Figure 89B). Other storage building designs with greater traffic should use an exterior prehung door complete with threshold and side and head jambs (see Figures 89A and 89C).

Figure 89D illustrates the installation of a metal framed window with nail-on flange. These windows are inexpensive, readily available, and relatively easy to install. Consult the manufacturer's installation instructions for precise step-by-step procedures.

Figure 89A - Service Door Jamb Detail

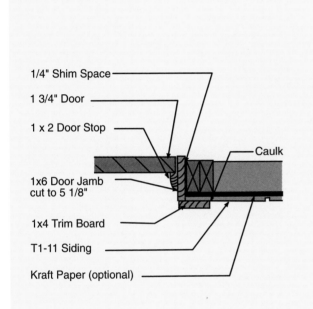

1/4" Shim Space
1 3/4" Door
1 x 2 Door Stop
Caulk
1x6 Door Jamb cut to 5 1/8"
1x4 Trim Board
T1-11 Siding
Kraft Paper (optional)

Figure 89B - Built On-Site Barn Door

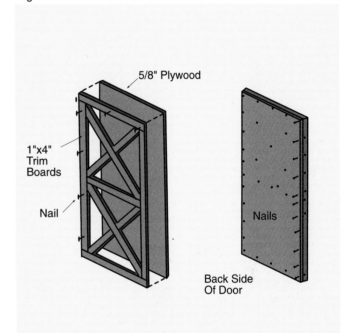

5/8" Plywood
1"x4" Trim Boards
Nail
Nails
Back Side Of Door

Figure 89C - Service Door Head

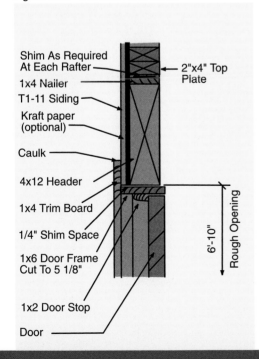

Shim As Required At Each Rafter
2"x4" Top Plate
1x4 Nailer
T1-11 Siding
Kraft paper (optional)
Caulk
4x12 Header
1x4 Trim Board
1/4" Shim Space
1x6 Door Frame Cut To 5 1/8"
1x2 Door Stop
Door
6'-10" Rough Opening

Figure 89D - Metal-Framed Window Installation

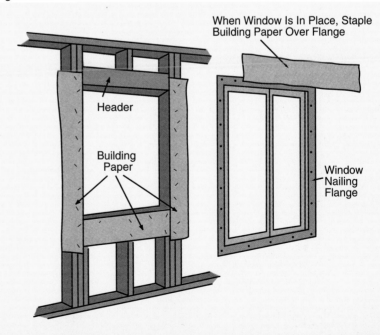

When Window Is In Place, Staple Building Paper Over Flange
Header
Building Paper
Window Nailing Flange

Once the roof sheathing, cornice trim, and fascia boards are in place, the roof shingles can be applied. See the shingle manufacturer's instructions on the bundle. Shingles chosen to harmonize with or match your home are recommended. Square butt shingles are 36" x 12" in size, have three tabs, and are normally laid with 5" exposed to the weather (see Figure 90A).

Start with 15# asphalt felt paper at the bottom edge of the roof. Lap each course 2". After the roofing felt is on, apply a starter course of shingles (shingles turned upside down), lapping over the eave and rake fascia 1/2" to provide a drip edge. Use four nails for each shingle and apply a Boston ridge at top that is made by cutting a shingle into thirds (see Figure 90E). Start at one end of the ridge and fasten with two nails to a shingle leaving a 5" exposure. Cut shingles with a utility knife. Metal drip edges are used in some regions.

For a simple-to-install storage building roof, use panel roofing (see Figure 90B). Be sure to overhang the eave by at least 2" and install a ridge cap. You can insert one or two translucent fiberglass roof panels between the solid metal roof panels to provide for natural lighting.

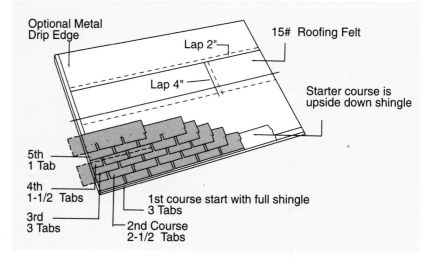

Figure 90A - Shingle Plan

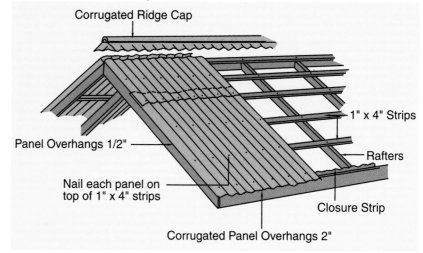

Figure 90B - Panel Roofing

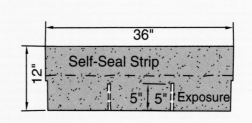

Figure 90C - Tab shingles are always applied so that a full tab is centered over a slot below. If length of roof requires a narrow piece to finish first course, start the second row with piece of same width. Continue alternating narrow pieces in each succeeding row.

Figure 90D - Shingle Ridge Detail

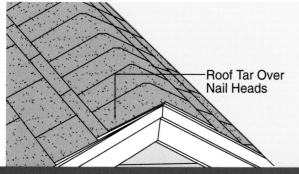

Roof Tar Over Nail Heads

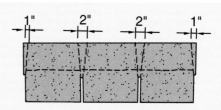

Figure 90E - To cut a shingle, score a line with your utility knife, then bend and snap off the piece. Make 3 hip or ridge shingles from one shingle.

Depending on how you are going to utilize your storage building, you might want to install electrical wiring. Two steps are almost mandatory if you plan to supply your storage building with electrical service and want to do the job yourself:

1. First check with your local building department and determine the code standards for your area. They will advise you regarding permit and inspection requirements. They will also advise you whether or not there are any requirements for using a professional electrician during wiring.

2. Consult with your local power company. They will inform you if you need a separate electrical service for your storage building. If you plan on running off existing home service, they will tell you if your home service can carry the additional load.

If you are allowed to use a branch circuit from your main panel, install an additional Ground Fault Circuit Interrupter (GFCI) type circuit breaker in your main circuit box and then use buried cable (Type UF cable for underground burial) to supply your storage building. Be certain that you bury the cable in an area that will not be disturbed by digging or other activity. Certain municipalities might not allow buried cable and will require a separate service installation.

You should install a main disconnect box for electrical service inside your storage building. Be sure not to exceed the total amperage rating of the box in your branch circuits. Inside the storage building, you can wire lighting and receptacles using either romex (Type NM cable) or metal sheathed cable (Type BX cable) depending upon your local code requirements. If you are wiring a moist area such as a greenhouse or cabana, use Type NMC cable or Type UM for extra protection against moisture. Also install GFCI receptacles in areas with excessive moisture. Consult your local building department for GFCI requirements and regulations.

Figure 91 - Electrical Wiring Options

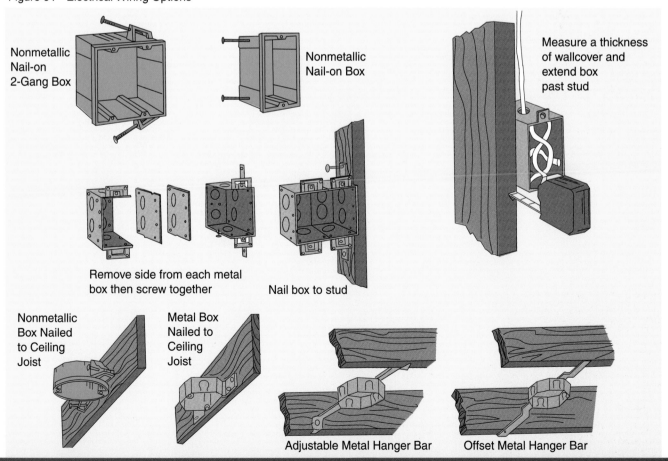

Nonmetallic Nail-on 2-Gang Box

Nonmetallic Nail-on Box

Measure a thickness of wallcover and extend box past stud

Remove side from each metal box then screw together

Nail box to stud

Nonmetallic Box Nailed to Ceiling Joist

Metal Box Nailed to Ceiling Joist

Adjustable Metal Hanger Bar

Offset Metal Hanger Bar

You can either finish the interior of your storage building with drywall or leave the wall studs exposed and use blocking to build shelving between the studs. Most storage builders will want to take advantage of the extra storage space afforded by the open wall sections. Use your imagination to create additional storage space by nailing or screwing 1x2 cleats to the studs and then installing extended horizontal shelving over the cleats.

If you elect to install 4'x8' drywall panels (also known as wallboard) in your storage building, study the illustrations below for suggestions on nailing or gluing drywall to wall studs.

A variety of fasteners are available for wallboard. Consult your local home center or building material supplier for suggestions. After you have installed the panels, you can tape and fill the joints with joint compound or simply cover the joints with tape if the final appearance is not a major concern.

Figure 92A - Nailing Wallboard

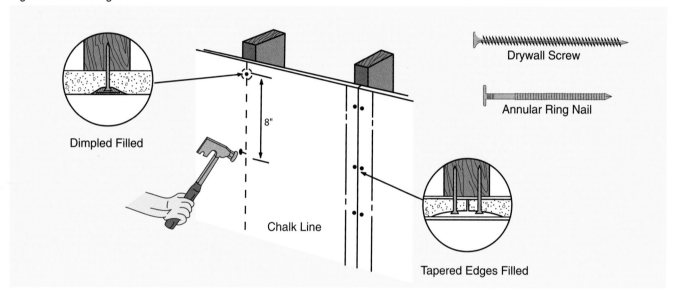

Figure 92B - Gluing Wallboard

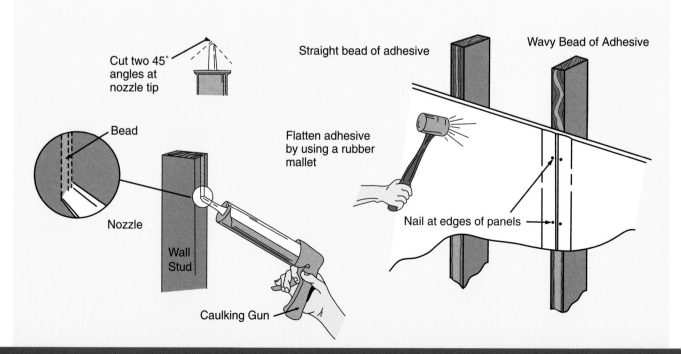

ADDING A RAMP TO YOUR BUILDING

An entry ramp makes life easier for you and your storage building. Instead of lugging heavy garden tools such as mowers or snow removal machines up and down from ground level to storage building level, use a ramp built from solid 2x material to improve accessibility. If your ramp will be over 3 feet in width, add an additional 2x vertical support to the center of the ramp. Nail the ramp decking to the ramp supports with 12d hot-dipped galvanized nails or use 3" decking screws.

Figure 93A - Design A

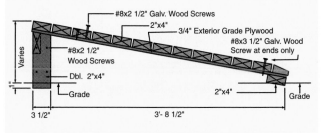

Side Elevation

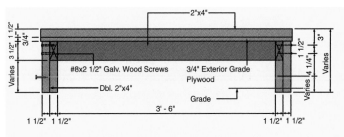

Back Side Elevation

Figure 93B - Design B

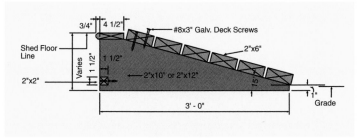

Side Elevation

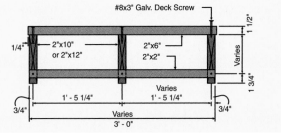

Back Side Elevation

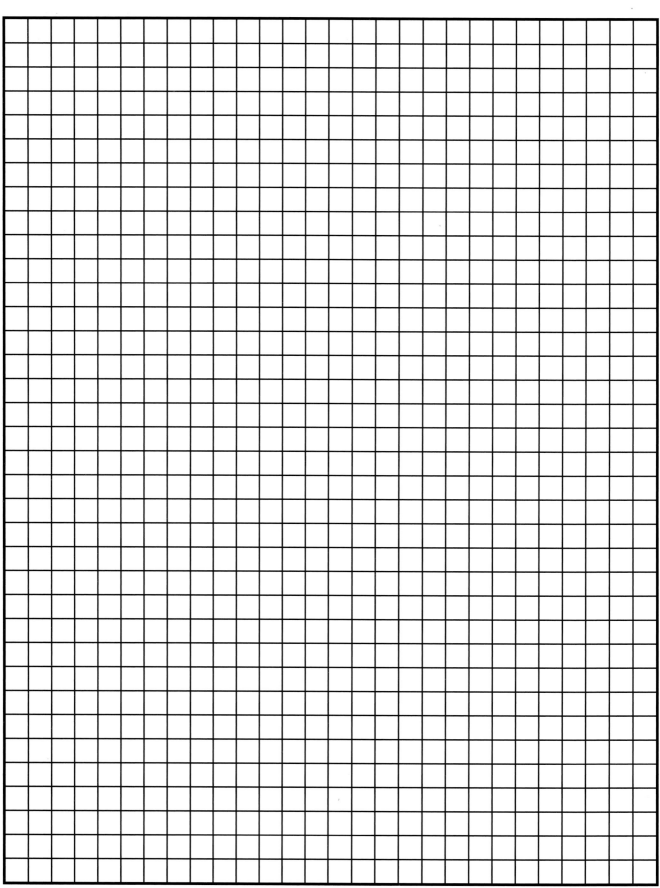

Scale: ¼" = 1'-0" per square

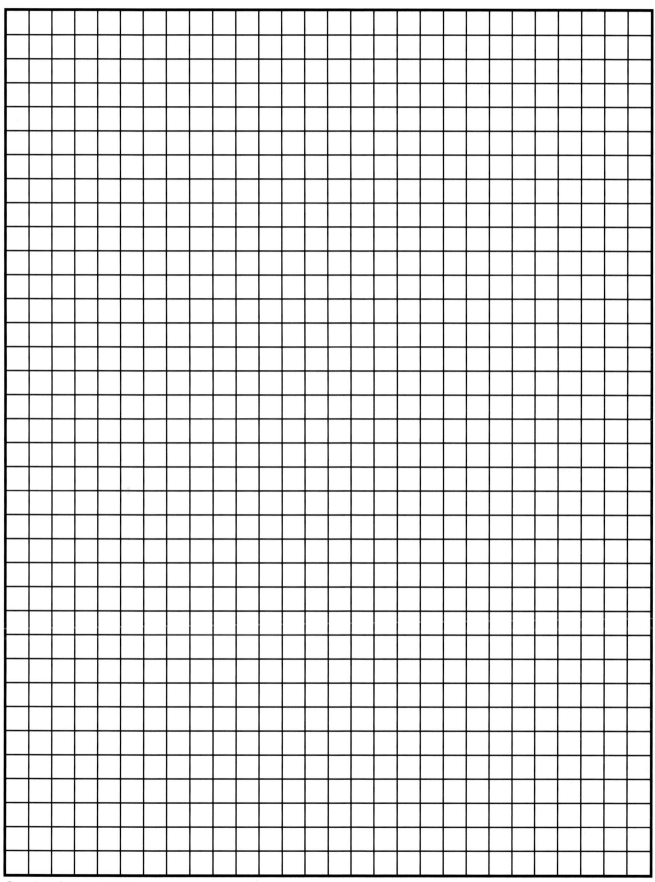

Scale: ¼" = 1'-0" per square

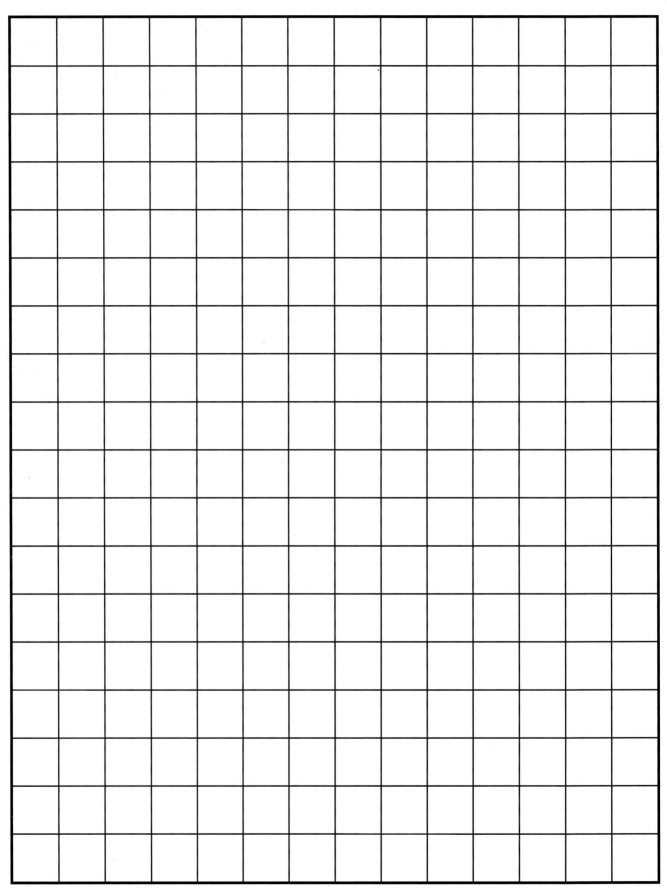

Scale: ½" = 1'-0" per square

READY TO START SERIOUS PLANNING?

Now that you have read this book from cover to cover, you're ready to start serious planning. As you can see, there are many details to consider, and they all tie together for successful completion of your storage building project.

If the procedures appear at first confusing, reread the information outlined in this book several times before deciding which phases of construction you want to handle yourself and which might require professional assistance.

Because drawing up your own plan from scratch can be time consuming and difficult for the inexperienced builder, you might want to make planning and cost estimating easier by selecting a design from those shown in this book.

You can order construction blueprints with complete material lists at your local Menards store. Simply visit the Building Materials Desk and a friendly building material team member will be happy to assist you. If after reviewing the blueprints you still have questions, talk them over with your building material associate. Most associates are familiar with construction and will be glad to help you.

The following pages include an assortment of pre-drawn storage building and deck plans. All blueprint plans include a complete material list, exterior elevations, sections and details, and step-by-step instructions for the successful completion of your storage building or deck project.

All blueprint plans include exterior elevations, sections and/or details, floor plans, foundation plans, rafter templates, and lumber lists.

NOTES

_____

_____

_____

_____

_____

_____

_____

_____

_____

_____

_____

FULLY DETAILED BLUEPRINTS AVAILABLE

for all deck and storage building designs featured in this publication.

Deck and Storage Building Blueprint Plans include the following:

- Floor plan and elevations
- Rafter or truss diagrams
- Wall framing and/or details
- A complete list of materials

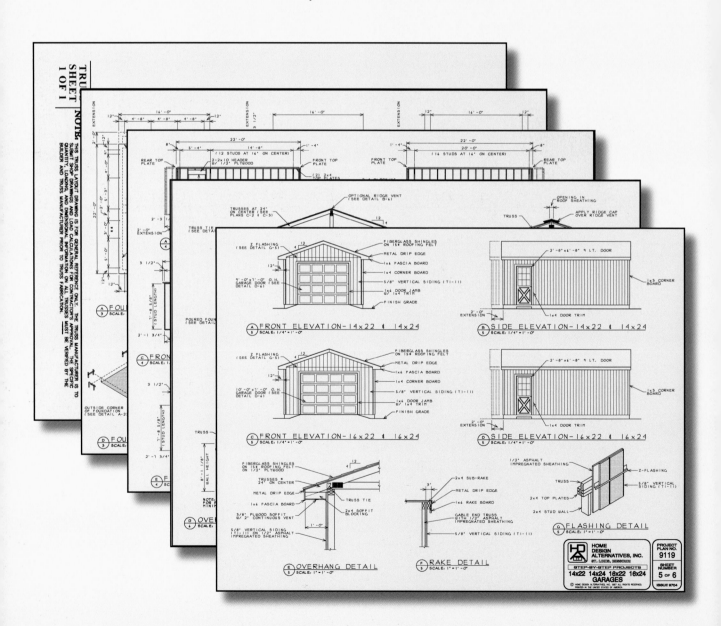

STORAGE BUILDINGS & DECK PLANS

Plan #M05-002D-3027

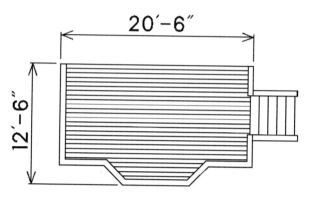

Bay Deck
With Railing

- Size - 20'-6" x 12'-6"
- Adds beauty and value to your home
- Unique layout with built-in bay
- Complete list of materials
- Step-by-step instructions

Plan #M05-002D-3023

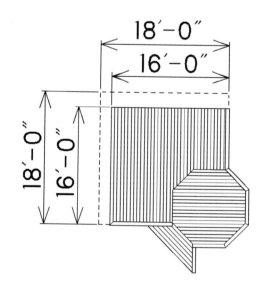

Deck With
Sunken Dining Area

- Two popular sizes -
  16' x 16'
  18' x 18'
- Unique sunken area adds interest to this deck
- Perfect addition to enhance outdoor entertaining
- Complete list of materials
- Step-by-step instructions

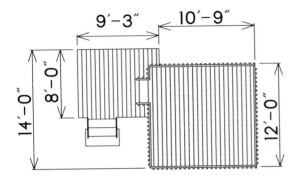

Split-Level Deck

- Overall size - 20' x 14'
  - lower deck - 9' x 8'
  - upper deck - 12' x 12'
- Can be built with standard lumber
- Adaptable to all grades
- Complete list of materials
- Step-by-step instructions

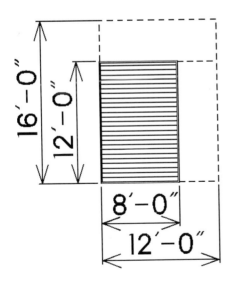

Easy Decks

- Three great sizes -
  - 8' x 12'
  - 12' x 12'
  - 12' x 16'
- Low cost construction
- Can be built with standard lumber
- Adaptable to all grades
- Complete list of materials
- Step-by-step instructions

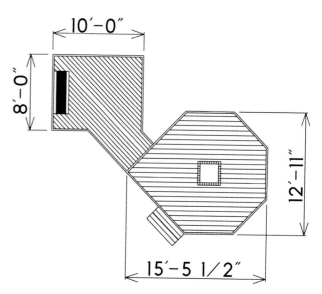

High-Low Deck

- Lower deck size - 15'-5 1/2" x 12'-11"
- Upper deck size - 10'-0" x 8'-0"
- Designed as an add-on to an existing deck or as a complete unit
- Benches can be arranged as needed
- Features a unique conversation area or fire pit
- Complete list of materials
- Step-by-step instructions

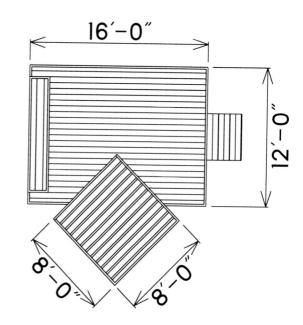

Two-Level Garden Deck

- Overall size - 16' x 19'
  - main deck - 16' x 12'
  - upper deck - 8' x 8'
- Unique design features decorative plant display area or sundeck
- Built-in seating
- Can be free-standing or attached
- Complete list of materials
- Step-by-step instructions

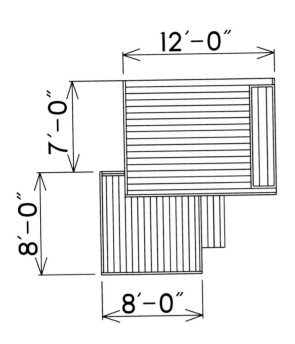

Two-Level Deck With Bench

- Overall size - 14' x 15'
  lower deck - 8' x 8'
  upper deck - 12' x 9'
- Unique, attractive design features two-level deck and bench
- Adds great value to your home
- Complete list of materials
- Step-by-step instructions

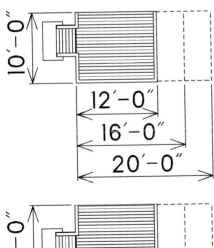

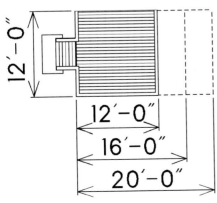

Expandable Decks

- Six popular sizes -

12' x 10'	12' x 12'
16' x 10'	16' x 12'
20' x 10'	20' x 12'

- Functional decks in a variety of sizes to fit your every need
- Complete list of materials
- Step-by-step instructions

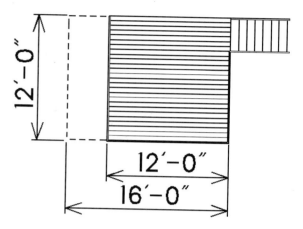

Raised Patio Decks

- Two popular sizes -
  - 12' x 12'
  - 16' x 12'
- Both decks can be constructed at any height
- Can be built to fit any lot situation
- Complete list of materials
- Step-by-step instructions

Plan #M05-002D-3004

Price Code P3

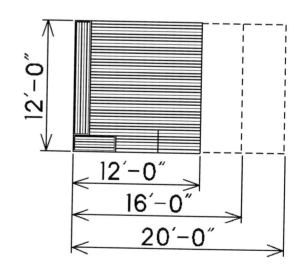

Low Patio Decks

- Three popular sizes -
  - 12' x 12'
  - 16' x 12'
  - 20' x 12'
- Built-in seating
- Perfect for entertaining
- Complete list of materials
- Step-by-step instructions

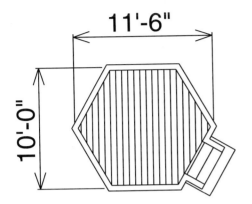

Hexagon Deck

- Size - 11'-6" x 10'-0"
- Free-standing design
- Attractive deck with a choice of two railing styles
- Simple construction - easy to build
- Complete list of materials
- Step-by-step instructions

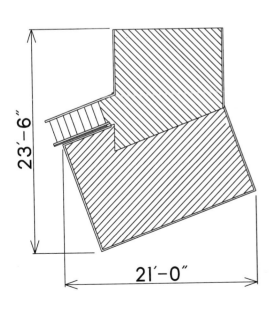

Two-Level Raised Deck

- Overall size - 21'-0" x 24'-0"
  lower deck - 18'-0" x 12'-0"
  upper deck - 12'-0" x 12'-9"
- Can be built at any height
- Adaptable to any lot situation
- Complete list of materials
- Step-by-step instructions

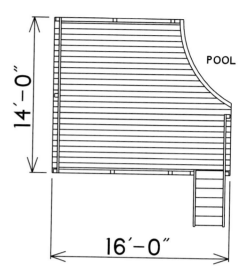

POOL

14'-0"

16'-0"

Pool Deck

- Size - 16' x 14'
- Can be built to fit any size pool
- Simple but sturdy design with built-in gate
- Makes cleaning and maintaining pool a breeze
- Complete list of materials
- Step-by-step instructions

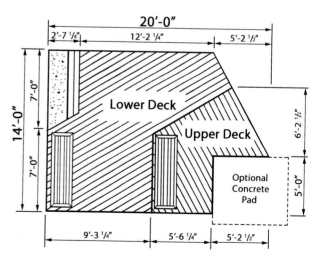

20'-0"

2'-7 1/4"   12'-2 1/4"   5'-2 1/2"

14'-0"

7'-0"

7'-0"

Lower Deck

Upper Deck

6'-2 1/2"

Optional Concrete Pad

5'-0"

9'-3 1/4"   5'-6 1/4"   5'-2 1/2"

Two-Level Spa Deck

- Overall size - 20'-0" x 14'-0"
  lower deck - 14'-9" x 14'-0"
  upper deck - 10'-8 3/4" x 11'-2 1/2"
- Designed for self-contained portable spas
- Free-standing or next to house
- Complete list of materials
- Step-by-step instructions

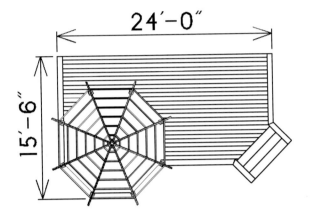

Deck With Gazebo

- Size - 24'-0" x 15'-6"
- Height floor to peak - 12'-2"
- Perfect for outdoor entertaining
- Gazebo adds unique flair to this deck
- Complete list of materials
- Step-by-step instructions

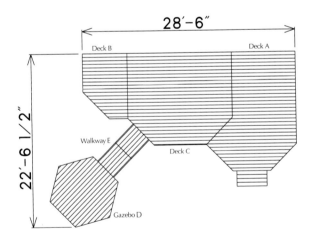

Tiered Deck With Gazebo

- Sizes -
  Overall area - 28'-6" x 22'-6 1/2"
  - Deck A - 9'-0" x 15'-6"
  - Deck B - 6'-6" x 8'-6"
  - Deck C - 14'-0" x 12'-0"
  - Gazebo D - 9'-6" x 8'-3" sided
  - Walkway E - 3'-0" x 7'-0"
- Complete list of materials
- Step-by-step instructions

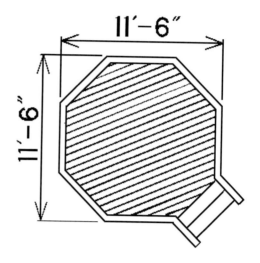

Octagon Gazebo

- Size - 11'-6" x 11'-6"
- Height floor to peak - 14'-7"
- Large gazebo has plenty of space for outdoor entertaining
- This attractive structure will complement any setting
- Complete list of materials
- Step-by-step instructions

Plan #M05-002D-3018

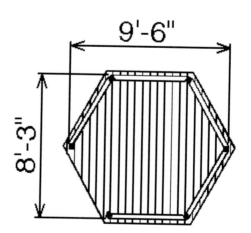

Six-Sided Gazebo

- Size - 8'-3" x 9'-6"
- Height floor to peak - 12'-10"
- Complements any setting
- Cozy gazebo is great for entertaining a small group
- Complete list of materials
- Step-by-step instructions

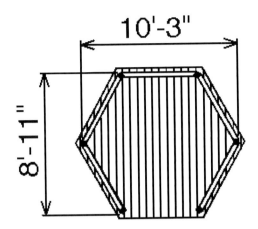

10'-3"

8'-11"

Six-Sided Gazebo

- Size - 10'-3" x 8'-11"
- Height from top of floor to peak - 10'-9"
- Ideal for small gatherings
- This traditional design will enhance any outdoor setting
- Complete list of materials
- Step-by-step instructions

8'-0"

10'-0"

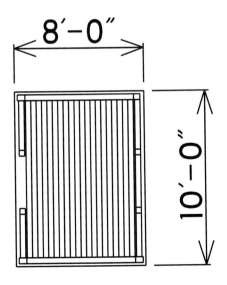

Four-Sided Gazebo

- Size - 8' x 10'
- Height from top of floor to peak - 11'
- Gable roof construction
- A unique and functional addition to your yard
- Adds additional shade and privacy for outdoor entertaining
- Complete list of materials
- Step-by-step instructions

Patio Covers - Roof/Sun Shade

- Patio roof size - 16' x 9'
- Sun shade size - 20' x 10'
- A unique and functional addition to your home
- Complete list of materials
- Step-by-step instructions

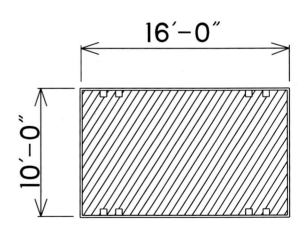

16´-0˝

10´-0˝

Shaded Deck

- Size - 16'-0" x 10'-0" x 9'-6" high
- Deck design has a sun-screen covering
- Enhance your outdoors with this shaded deck
- Complete list of materials
- Step-by-step instructions

Pri... Plan

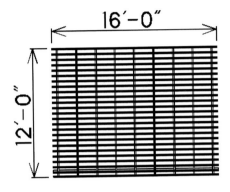

Easy Patio Cover

- Size - 16' x 12'
- Attractive patio cover features a sun-screen covering
- Add value and beauty to your home
- Complete list of materials
- Step-by-step instructions

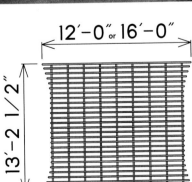

Patio Covers

- Two sizes -
  12' x 13'-2 1/2"
  16' x 13'-2 1/2"
- Designed to cover an existing deck or patio or used as a pavilion
- Can be built with standard lumber
- Plan includes an alternate bench design
- Complete list of materials
- Step-by-step instructions

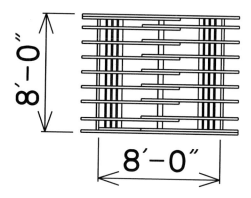

Garden Entryway

- Size - 8' x 8'
- Height peak to grade - 10'-10"
- Unique, attractive design that will complement either your garden or home
- Simple construction
- Complete list of materials
- Step-by-step instructions

Plan #M05-002D-3013

Price Code P4

Deck Enhancements

- Four unique designs -
  - Planter box - 2'-0" x 2'-0"
  - Decorative screen - 7'-0" x 5'-6"
  - Bench - 6'-0" x 1'-8"
  - End table - 2'-6" x 1'-5"
- Adds to any existing deck
- Can be free-standing or attached to your deck
- Complete list of materials
- Step-by-step instructions

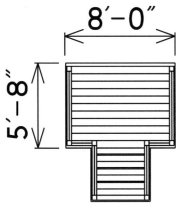

Entry Porches

- Size - 8'-0" x 5'-8"
- Two popular styles - contemporary and colonial
- Attractive designs to fit any type of home
- Can be free-standing or attached
- Adaptable for trailer or home use
- Complete list of materials
- Step-by-step instructions

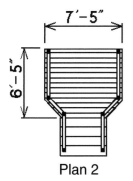

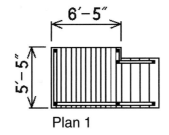

Plan 2

Plan 1

Entry Porches

- Two popular styles -
  Plan 1 - 6'-5" x 5'-5"
  Plan 2 - 7'-5" x 6'-5"
- Functional porches that enhance any entrance
- Complete list of materials
- Step-by-step instructions

To order this plan, visit the Menards Building Materials Desk.

113

Plan #M05-002D-3022

Price Code P3

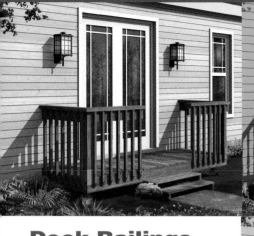

Deck Railings

- Five styles to choose from
- Can easily be added to your existing deck
- Complement any design
- Easily adaptable to any outdoor structure
- Complete list of materials
- Step-by-step instructions

Plan #M05-002D-3003

Price Code P5

3 Bridges

- Three styles and sizes -
  Plan 1 - 18'-0" x 4'-11"
  Plan 2 - 13'-5" x 4'-11"
  Plan 3 - 11'-0" x 4'-11"
- Enhance your outdoors
- Complete list of materials
- Step-by-step instructions

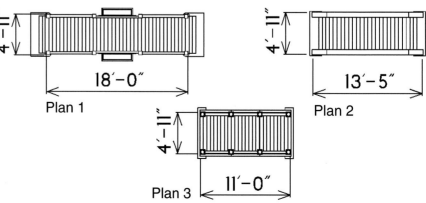

114

To order this plan, visit the Menards Building Materials Desk.

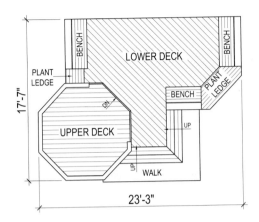

Large Deck
With Multiple Levels

- Size - 23'-3" x 17'-7"
- Plenty of space is offered for grand outdoor living
- Built-in benches and a plant ledge provide beauty and function
- Complete list of materials
- Step-by-step instructions

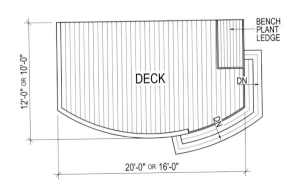

Low-Level Deck

- Sizes -
    20' x 12'
    20' x 10'
    16' x 12'
    16' x 10'
- Enjoy the outdoors with this beautiful backyard addition
- Complete list of materials
- Step-by-step instructions

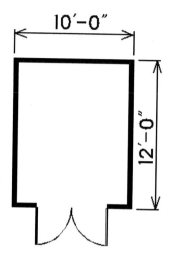

Yard Barn With Loft Storage

- Size - 10' x 12'
- Wood floor on 4x4 runners
- Height floor to peak - 10'-7"
- Ceiling height - 6'-11"
- 6'-0" x 6'-2" double-door for easy access
- Loft provides additional storage area
- Attractive styling is suitable for any yard
- Complete list of materials
- Step-by-step instructions

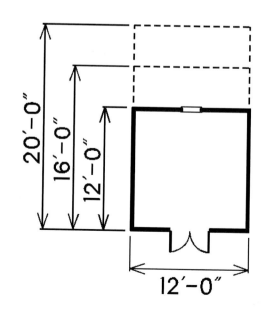

Barn Storage Buildings With Loft

- Three popular sizes -
  12' x 12'   12' x 16'   12' x 20'
- Wood floor on concrete pier foundation or concrete floor
- Height floor to peak - 12'-10"
- Ceiling height - 7'-4"
- 4'-0" x 6'-8" double-door for easy access
- Complete list of materials
- Step-by-step instructions

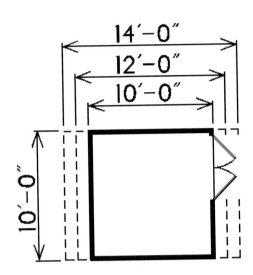

Garden Storage Buildings With Clerestory

- Three popular sizes -
  10' x 10'   12' x 10'   14' x 10'
- Wood floor on 4x6 runners
- Height floor to peak - 10'-11"
- Rear wall height - 7'-3"
- 5'-0" x 6'-9" double-door for easy access
- Clerestory windows for added light
- Complete list of materials
- Step-by-step instructions

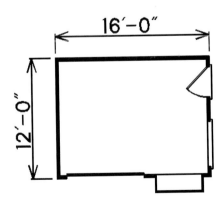

Convenience Storage Building

- Size - 16' x 12'
- Concrete floor
- Height floor to peak - 12'-4 1/2"
- Ceiling height - 8'
- 8' x 7' overhead door
- Ideal for lawn equipment or small boat storage
- Oversized windows brighten interior
- Complete list of materials
- Step-by-step instructions

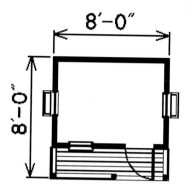

Exciting Playhouse

- Size - 8' x 8'
- Wood floor on 4x4 runners
- Height floor to peak - 9'-2"
- Ceiling height - 6'-1"
- 2' deep porch
- Attractive window boxes
- Includes operable windows
- Complete list of materials
- Step-by-step instructions

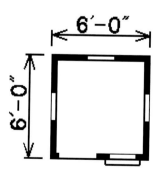

Children's Playhouse

- Size - 6' x 6'
- Wood floor on gravel base
- Height floor to peak - 7'-2"
- Wall height - 4'-4"
- Plenty of windows brighten interior
- Beautiful Victorian style
- Attractive gabled doorway and window box
- Complete list of materials
- Step-by-step instructions

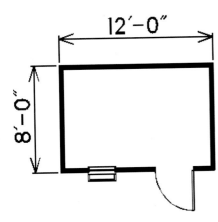

Gable Storage Building/Playhouse

- Size - 12' x 8'
- Wood floor on 4x4 runners
- Height floor to peak - 10'-5"
- Ceiling height - 8'
- 3'-0" x 6'-8" dutch door
- Shutters and window box create a charming facade
- Complete list of materials
- Step-by-step instructions

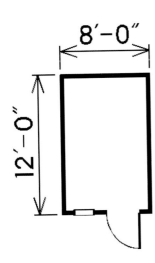

Playhouse/Storage Building

- Size - 8' x 12'
- Wood floor on concrete piers or concrete floor
- Height floor to peak - 10'-6"
- Ceiling height - 7'
- 3' x 6' door
- Ideal playhouse in summer
- Storage building in the off season
- Complete list of materials
- Step-by-step instructions

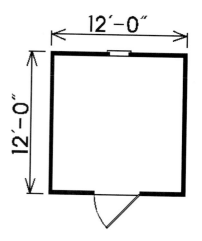

Storage Building With Playhouse Loft

- Size - 12' x 12' with 2'-8" deep balcony
- Wood floor on concrete piers or concrete floor
- Height floor to peak - 14'-1"
- Ceiling height - 7'-4"
- 4'-0" x 6'-10" door
- Loft above can be used as playhouse for children
- Complete list of materials
- Step-by-step instructions

Mini Barns

- Four popular sizes -
  8' x 8'   8' x 10'   8' x 12'   8' x 16'
- Wood floor on 4x4 runners
- Height floor to peak - 7'-6"
- Ceiling height - 6'
- 4' x 6' double-door for easy access
- Attractive styling for any backyard
- Complete list of materials
- Step-by-step instructions

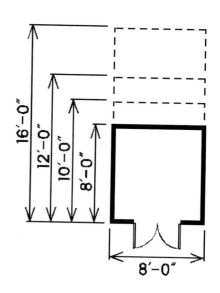

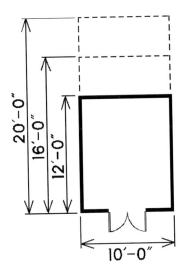

Yard Barns

- Three popular sizes -
  10' x 12'   10' x 16'   10' x 20'
- Wood floor on 4x4 runners
- Height floor to peak - 8'-4 1/2"
- Ceiling height - 6'-4"
- 4'-0" x 6'-4" double-door for easy access
- Ample storage area for lawn or garden equipment
- Complete list of materials
- Step-by-step instructions

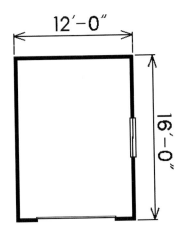

Barn Storage Building With Overhead Door

- Size - 12' x 16'
- Concrete floor
- Height floor to peak - 12'-5"
- Ceiling height - 8'
- 8' x 7' overhead door for easy entry with large equipment
- Complete list of materials
- Step-by-step instructions

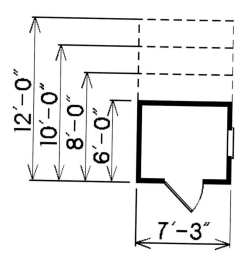

Mini-Barn Storage Buildings

- Four popular sizes -
  7'-3" x 6'   7'-3" x 8'   7'-3" x 10'   7'-3" x 12'
- Wood floor on 4x6 runners or concrete floor
- Height floor to peak - 9'
- Ceiling height - 7'-4"
- 3'-0" x 6'-8" door
- Attractive styling with gambrel roof
- Complete list of materials
- Step-by-step instructions

Plan #M05-002D-4508

Price Code P5

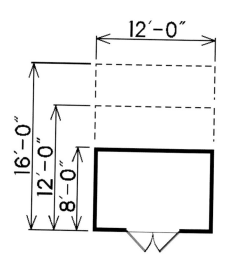

Barn Storage Buildings

- Three popular sizes -
  12' x 8'   12' x 12'   12' x 16'
- Wood floor on concrete pier foundation
  or concrete floor
- Height floor to peak - 9'-10"
- Ceiling height - 7'-10"
- 5'-6" x 6'-8" double-door for easy access
- Complete list of materials
- Step-by-step instructions

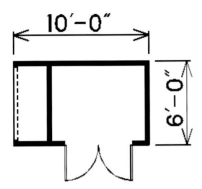

Storage Building With Log Bin

- Size - 10' x 6'
- Wood floor on gravel base
- Height floor to peak - 9'-7"
- Ceiling height - 6'-7"
- 5'-0" x 6'-9" double-door for easy access
- Log storage area - 2'-6" x 6'-0"
- Complete list of materials
- Step-by-step instructions

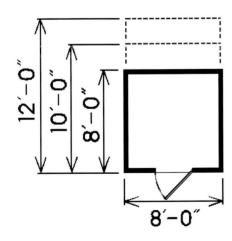

Gable Storage Buildings

- Three popular sizes -
  8' x 8'   8' x 10'   8' x 12'
- Wood floor on concrete footings
- Height floor to peak - 9'-1"
- Wall height - 6'-7"
- Circle-top window adds interest and light
- Complete list of materials
- Step-by-step instructions

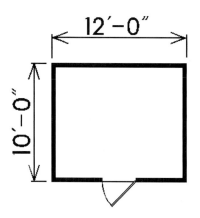

Gable Storage Building With Cupola

- Size - 12' x 10'
- Wood floor on concrete piers or concrete floor
- Height floor to peak - 9'-8"
- Ceiling height - 7'-4"
- 3'-0" x 6'-8" door
- Made of cedar plywood with battens
- Complete list of materials
- Step-by-step instructions

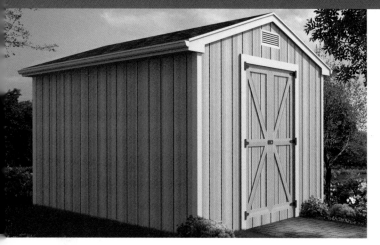

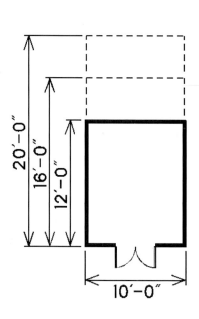

Gable Storage Buildings

- Three popular sizes -
  10' x 12'   10' x 16'   10' x 20'
- Wood floor on 4x4 runners
- Height floor to peak - 8'-8 1/2"
- Ceiling height - 7'
- 4'-0" x 6'-4" double-door for easy access
- Complete list of materials
- Step-by-step instructions

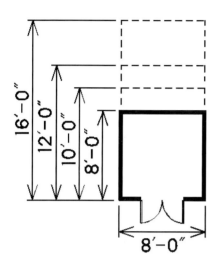

Gable Storage Buildings

- Four popular sizes -
  - 8' x 8'   8' x 10'   8' x 12'   8' x 16'
- Wood floor on 4x4 runners
- Height floor to peak - 8'-4 1/2"
- Ceiling height - 7'
- 4'-0" x 6'-5" double-door for easy access
- Economical and easy to build storage building
- Complete list of materials
- Step-by-step instructions

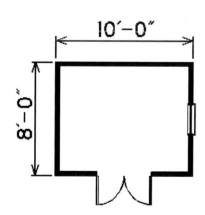

Salt Box Storage Building

- Size - 10' x 8'
- Wood floor on 4x4 runners
- Height floor to peak - 9'-6"
- Front wall height - 8'
- 4'-0" x 6'-8" double-door for easy access
- Window adds light to space
- Complete list of materials
- Step-by-step instructions

Salt Box Storage Buildings

- Three popular sizes -
  - 8' x 8'   12' x 8'   16' x 8'
- Wood floor on gravel base or concrete floor
- Height floor to peak - 8'-2"
- Front wall height - 7'
- 6'-0" x 6'-5" double-door for easy access
- Complete list of materials
- Step-by-step instructions

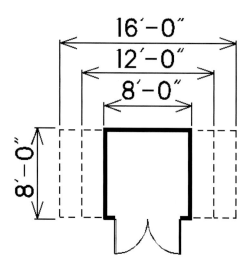

Deluxe Cabana

- Size - 11'-0" x 13'-6"
- Concrete floor
- Height floor to peak - 11'-7"
- Ceiling height - 8'
- Unique roof design with skylight
- Convenient dressing room and servicing area
- Perfect storage for poolside furniture and equipment
- Complete list of materials
- Step-by-step instructions

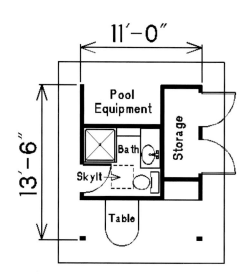

Garden Storage Building

- Size - 12' x 10'
- Wood floor on gravel base
- Height floor to peak - 9'-9"
- Rear wall height - 7'-1 1/2"
- Features skylight windows for optimal plant growth
- Ample room for tool and lawn equipment storage
- Complete list of materials
- Step-by-step instructions

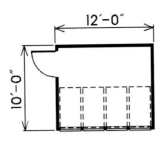

Greenhouse

- Size - 8' x 12'
- Gravel floor with concrete foundation wall
- Height foundation to peak - 8'-3"
- An attractive addition to any yard
- Store lawn and garden tools right at hand
- Complete list of materials
- Step-by-step instructions

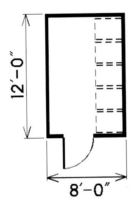

Garden Storage Building

- Size - 10' x 10'
- Wood floor on 4x4 runners
- Height floor to peak - 11'-3 1/2"
- Left wall height - 8'
- Wonderful complement to any backyard
- Perfect space for lawn equipment or plants and flowers
- Plenty of windows for gardening year-round
- Complete list of materials
- Step-by-step instructions

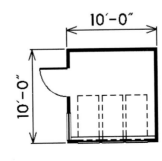

Plan Number	Price Code	Page	Plan Number	Price Code	Page
M05-002D-3000	P6	108	M05-002D-3029	P6	107
M05-002D-3001	P6	107	M05-002D-4500	P5	126
M05-002D-3002	P4	103	M05-002D-4501	P5	116
M05-002D-3003	P5	114	M05-002D-4502	P5	121
M05-002D-3004	P3	104	M05-002D-4503	P5	125
M05-002D-3005	P4	104	M05-002D-4504	P5	124
M05-002D-3006	P4	106	M05-002D-4505	P4	118
M05-002D-3007	P5	103	M05-002D-4506	P6	117
M05-002D-3008	P5	110	M05-002D-4507	P5	127
M05-002D-3009	P4	102	M05-002D-4508	P5	122
M05-002D-3010	P5	102	M05-002D-4509	P5	123
M05-002D-3011	P3	101	M05-002D-4510	P5	122
M05-002D-3012	P3	113	M05-002D-4511	P5	124
M05-002D-3013	P4	112	M05-002D-4512	P4	119
M05-002D-3014	P4	111	M05-002D-4513	P5	127
M05-002D-3015	P4	111	M05-002D-4514	P5	120
M05-002D-3016	P5	101	M05-002D-4515	P5	117
M05-002D-3017	P5	112	M05-002D-4516	P5	123
M05-002D-3018	P5	108	M05-002D-4517	P4	118
M05-002D-3019	P5	106	M05-002D-4518	P6	126
M05-002D-3020	P5	105	M05-002D-4519	P5	125
M05-002D-3021	P4	105	M05-002D-4520	P5	116
M05-002D-3022	P3	114	M05-002D-4521	P5	121
M05-002D-3023	P5	100	M05-002D-4522	P5	119
M05-002D-3024	P4	110	M05-002D-4523	P5	127
M05-002D-3025	P5	109	M05-002D-4524	P5	120
M05-002D-3026	P5	109	M05-107D-3001	P5	115
M05-002D-3027	P4	100	M05-107D-3002	P4	115
M05-002D-3028	P3	113			